THE MAYLORD ORCHARDS HEREFORD

L ocated in the heart of Hereford is the award winning Maylord Orchards Shopping Centre, a development designed to meet the needs of visitors and local shoppers alike. The Maylord Orchards has brought to this historical and picturesque city a host of well-known faces.

The Centre has been designed to blend with the important architectural features of the city and clearly complements the surrounding buildings.

Published by Revelsone Publishing Ltd.
on behalf of Hereford City Council

K.F. Rayner,
City Health & Leisure Officer

Phototypsetting by Mane Image Ltd; Leicester

Printed in Great Britain by
Ebenezer Baylis Ltd, Worcester
© Revelstone Publishing Ltd 1989

ISBN 1 871817 20 X paperback
ISBN 1 871817 25 O hardback

Hereford 800

a celebration

The first Charter

Written by Sue Hubbard

1189

The Richard I charter is very small compared with later charters, measuring only 140 x 118 cms. It is written on parchment (sheepskin) and the language is Latin, as is all the city's charters until 1836.

▽

Originally, the charter was authenticated by having the Great Seal attached to it. This royal seal has from the time of William the Conqueror traditionally shown the sovereign on one side enthroned as ruler, the source of justice and authority, and on the other armed and mounted, showing his readiness to defend his realm against the enemy. The seal has been lost from this, like many of the other early charters, as the beeswax from which seals are made is brittle and easily broken.

▽

The clauses of the charter may seem few and simple, but they laid the foundation for Hereford's independence as an incorporated borough, which was to reach its culmination and completion in the charter of Elizabeth I.

▽

By granting the citizens the right to hold their town by payment of £40 direct to the exchequer, the King freed them from the county administration, as they no longer had to pay to the county sheriff the usual sums due to the crown. They were also made independent in legal matters as the sheriff no longer had the right to interfere in cases arising in the city courts. At the same time, the charter confirmed the ancient ▷ rights and customs enjoyed by the citizens, giving them protection against later interference from outside, and showed the King's trust by making them responsible for their own defence, in the rebuilding and maintenance of the city walls. ▷

A question which is often asked is why the charter speaks of "Hereford in Wales?" Various explanations have been given - the clerks drawing up the charter in far-off Westminster were not sure where Hereford was, or the border was further east than it is now, putting Hereford into Wales. The answer probably falls between the two.

▽

In 1189 the border had not been definitely drawn: the great Marcher Lords were still busy with their task of creating peace in the frontier zone between Wales and England, and Hereford was very much a frontier town. In the The Domesday Book the old Welsh Kingdom of Archenfield had been shown as a semi-autonomous district, still subject to its own Celtic law and custom. Many Herefordians were Welsh-speaking; in 1390 the villagers of Garway complained that their local priest was incapable of hearing their confession since he was English and they spoke only Welsh. All these uncertainties and confusions probably contributed to that curious phrase in the charter. □

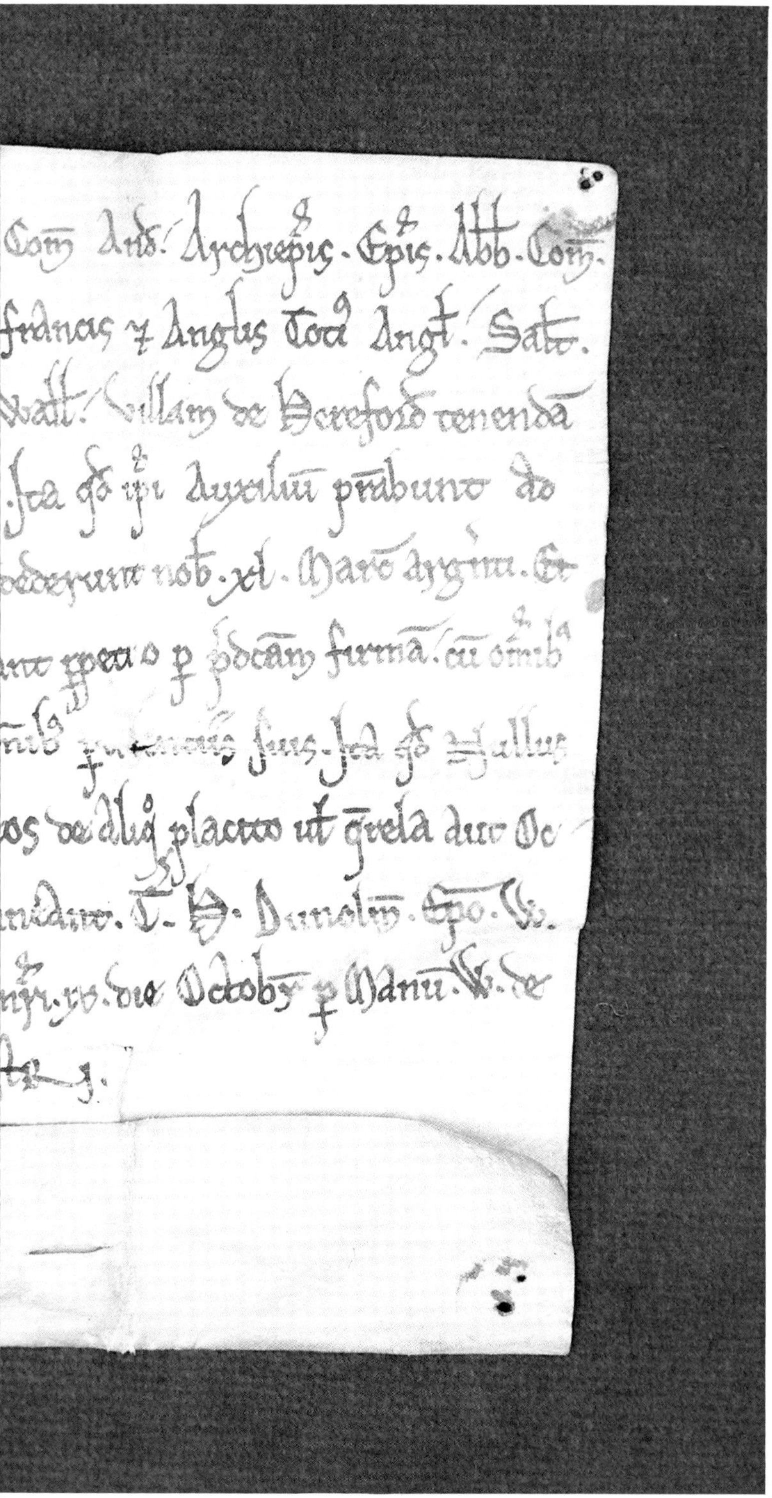

TRANSLATION

Richard by the grace of God King of England Duke of Normandy and Aquitane and Count of Anjou, to the archbishops, bishops, abbots, earls, barons, justices, sheriffs, ministers, and all his faithful subjects both French and English throughout England, greeting. Know that we have granted to our citizens of Hereford in Wales the town of Hereford to hold for ever for £40 to be paid yearly to the Exchequer. So that they shall give help in fortifying the town. And they have given us 40 marks of silver for this grant. And so we order that they shall have and hold the said town for ever for the said rent with all its liberties and free customs with all its apurtenances. So that none of our sheriffs shall impose his administration on them in any plea or suit or dispute or in any matter appertaining to the town.

Witnesses: Henry Bishop of Durham, William of St. John. Given at Westminister in the first year of our reign, 9 October by the hand of William de Longchamp Bishop elect of Ely, our Chancellor. □

The fee farm rent of £40, with other Crown rents, was sold off by Oliver Cromwell's commissioners in 1649. It eventually passed to the Merchant Taylor's Company, to whom it is still paid each year by Hereford City Council.

▷   △

Welcome

Gateway to the Welsh Marches, the City of Hereford has had a turbulent past stretching back over 1,300 years. It was one of the principal towns of the Saxon kingdom of Mercia, with the diocese being founded in AD 676. This strategic city was one of the sixteen shire towns ranked as Cities in the Domesday Book. Evidence of the very early formal plan and successive defences can still be seen today.

In 1189, Richard I granted Hereford's first Charter giving the citizens the right to hold their town by payment of £40 direct to the Exchequer. Eight hundred years on, Hereford now celebrates in style. A full programme of events arranged by community groups with the support of the council will provide the residents and visitors alike with the opportunity to participate in our 'Birthday Party.'

Hereford today is a thriving city, one of the fastest growing in Europe; looking to the future as well as reflecting on its historic past. Join us in 1989 and enjoy this book, wirtten by people in Hereford for the people of Hereford and all those who love this historic City.

CLLR. B.C. BALDWIN
MAYOR MAY 1988 - MAY 1989

CLLR. J.W. NEWMAN
MAYOR MAY 1989 - MAY 1990

Index

Editor: Ann Sandford

The production of this souvenir book has been made possible by the generous support of the organisations advertising within. We thank them for their assistance, and commend them to our readers. The range of their activities is a good indicator of the complex nature of our society, and in particular of our city. We hope you will agree that these advertisements add to the value of this book, which will be a source of pleasure and reference.

Barclays Bank Plc

Bay Horse Motors Ltd

British Gas Plc

H.P. Bulmer Drinks Ltd

The Business Promotion Centre

Denco Ltd

Godsell's (Hereford) Ltd

The Green Dragon Hotel

The Hereford Bookseller

Hereford Cathedral School

Hereford City Council - Technical Services

Hereford City Council - Health & Leisure

Hereford Fastenings. Co.

Hereford Industrial Supply Co. Ltd

Hereford Market Auctioneers Ltd

Hereford Moat House

Herefordshire Technical College

Inco Alloys Ltd

Lloyds Bank Plc

The Marches

Maylord Orchards

Melcon (Hereford)

Midland Red West Ltd

Morbaine Ltd

Oswin & Co. Ltd

Penn Travel Centre

Reed Newspapers - The Hereford Times

The Royal Bank of Scotland Plc

Sun Valley Poultry Ltd

SPEEDS' MAP OF HEREFORD 1610

8

THE EARLY CITY

The earliest permanent settlements in Herefordshire were Iron Age hill forts such as the one at Credenhill some 8 km west of Hereford. This was probably the administrative centre of the Decangi, a tribe which occupied Herefordshire and the surrounding areas between about 500 B.C. and the coming of the Romans.

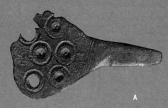

The Romans replaced the Iron Age capital with a small town at the bottom of the hill at Kenchester. This walled town is now a grass covered field, but excavations earlier in the present century uncovered the mosaic pavements which are now displayed in the Broad street museum.

It was some 250 years after the end of the Roman occupation of the country that the See of Hereford was founded in AD 676 although the origins of Hereford as a religious centre may pre-date the foundation of the diocese. St. Guthlac's collegiate establishment on Castle Green may well have been founded before the beginning of the 8th century as a religious settlement associated with the spring which later, as St. Ethelbert's Well, was said to have miraculous powers.

The earliest traces of occupation so far found in the city area were two grain-drying ovens built of re-used Roman altars and dated to the late 7th or 8th centuries. By the mid 8th century it is suggested that, apart from the two religious establishments, Hereford would only have comprised a few houses close to the cathedral and overlooking the main ford across the river Wye.

The late 8th and early 9th centuries were a period of growth for the city. Either Offa, during his long reign as King of Mercia, or possibly one of the minor kings who followed

north from the river, shows some evidence of deliberate planning. The main east-west street crossed the northern part of the cathedral close. The western part is now King Street and St. Nicholas Street, and the eastern section survives as Castle Street. Broad Street, the main north-south road, would

further to the south-east, surrounded by the city cemetery. The south-western quadrant was apparently a marshy area which was probably not settled until after a permanent bridge had been built.

Archaeological excavations have provided some indication of the lay-out of the houses in this early town. The average plot was about 18m square and each contained a single-storey building about 10m long and 6m wide, with a central passage dividing the building into two rooms. They were built of timber with the posts put directly into the ground and had earthen floors and a central hearth. The walls were probably covered in daub and the roofs would have been thatched. There would have been sufficient ground within each plot for some livestock or for cultivation. The roads separating the plots were laid with river pebbles and were about 4m wide.

SILVER RING BROOCH C. 1270-1330
THIS BROOCH WAS ON SHOW IN THE AGE OF CHIVALRY EXHIBITION AT THE ROYAL ACADEMY LONDON, IN 1987 AND IS THE FIRST OF ITS TYPE TO BE FOUND IN SOUTHERN ENGLAND. DISCOVERED DURING EXCAVATIONS AT BERRINGTON STREET, HEREFORD IN 1976, NOW ON SHOW IN THE CITY MUSEUM, BROAD STREET, HEREFORD.

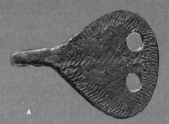

The earliest cathedral was probably also built of timber and would have been very small compared with the present building. It was not until the early 9th century that it was re-built in stone and even that structure has now totally disappeared.

him, may have been responsible for this expansion from a religious centre with a few houses to a planned royal town. The beginning of Offa's reign was troubled, but in AD 760 the English defeated the Welsh at the Battle of Hereford and it must have been shortly after that event that the negotiated frontier of Offa's Dyke was built some 15km west of the city.

The late 8th or early 9th century Saxon town, forming a narrow rectangle stretching

have continued down to the ford across the river in front of the Bishop's Palace gardens. A series of parallel streets, running northwards from the east-west thoroughfare, completed the embryonic city. Berrington Street, Aubrey Street and Church Street are present-day reminders of this 1200 year old example of town planning.

The cathedral precinct would have occupied the south-eastern quadrant with St. Guthlac's

The remains of Mercian Hereford are now completely buried underneath the ground, but the street plan, laid out some two to three hundred years before the Norman Conquest, remains as a visible reminder of the historic design of the early city

A) 11TH CENTURY BRONZE GARTER HOOKS
B) SAXON BONE COMB

THE CATHEDRAL AND CITY CHURCHES

Hereford Cathedral, built on a gravel terrace overlooking the early ford across the River Wye and adjoining the main crossroads of the Saxon burh, has always occupied a central position in the city demonstrating the open nature of the site when it was first founded in AD 676

The first cathedral was doubtless built of timber and was replaced around AD 829 by a stone building erected by Milfrith, King of Mercia in commemoration of the many miracles at the tomb of St. Ethelbert who was murdered at Sutton, near Hereford, in 792. This building was replaced by Bishop Athelstan in the early 11th century, only to be destroyed by the Wesh in 1055.

The destruction must have been complete for a new Norman building was gradually erected between 1080 and 1140, much of which still remains in the nave and south transept. Work continued throughout the centuries with the Lady Chapel, built in the early 13th century; the north transept in the later 13th century; the central and western towers in the early 1300's; the Chapter House later in the century, and additions including the bishop's Cloister and the College of the Vicar's

Choral during the 15th century.

Apart from the demolition of the Chapter house in the 17th century and the loss of Robert de Losinga's 11th century chapel in 1737, the most serious event to affect the cathedral was on April 17th, 1786 when the west tower, the west front, and the whole of the adjoining parts of the nave and aisles all fell down. The reconstruction and rebuilding by Wyatt included the present triforium and clerestorey and a plain west face. The existing west face, designed by Oldrid Scott, was built early in the present century.

BLACKFRIARS PREACHING CROSS

Much of the work was paid for by the pilgrims, who came first to the shrine of St Ethelbert, and later because of miracles which were said to be worked at the tomb of Bishop Thomas Cantilupe whose bones were brought back from Italy where he died in 1282. The magnificence of the rich 12th century ball-flower ornamentation on the central tower is a testimony to the generosity of these early pilgrims to Hereford.

The cathedral has two unique treasures - the renowned Chained Library, containing some 1500 chained books dating back to the 9th century, the largest such collection in the world; and the Mappa Mundi, a late 13th century map of the known world drawn by Richard de Haldingham. The latter has recently had much national publicity due to proposals by the Dean and Chapter to sell it by auction to raise funds for the Cathedral. Revised proposals indicate that it may well stay in the city and, hopefully become a focal point for modern-day pilgrims.

There was only one church built within the limits of the Saxon city, St. Nicholas', which stood in the middle of the road at the northern end of Bridge Street until it was taken down in ▷

1841 and replaced with a new church outside the City Wall. Two churches were built in the Norman market place - All Saints and St. Peter's - and both survive, their spires making a significant contribution to the visual landscape of the city.

The Civil War of 1645 was responsible for the loss of the two parish churches built outside the medieval city wall. St. Martin's, to the south of the river close to the bridge, was eventually replaced in 1845 on the new site further to the south, but St. Owen's, just outside the gate of the same name, was never rebuilt, the parish being combined with St. Peter's.

In addition to the parish churches there were three monastic establishments in the city, St. Guthlac's was the oldest, originally on Castle Green but moved to Commercial Road about 1144. After the dissolution of the monasteries the site was used for the County Goal which in turn was demolished and the area is now the bus station. The Franciscan Grey Friars had an establishment outside Friars' Gate by 1250, but all above ground traces have now disappeared, and the Dominican Black Friars eventually settled outside Widemarsh Gate in the early 14th century. The remains of part of the cloistral alley and the magnificent and unique Preaching Cross stand behind Coingsby's Hospital which itself includes the Chapel of the Knights Hospitallers. The Knights Templars also had a chapel in Hereford - a round church similar to the one in Ludlow Castle - now lost underneath the junction of Ledbury Road and St. Owen Street. Close by, in the side wall of one of the almshouses, is a stone tympanum, with an elaborate carving of Christ in Majesty, which may well have come from this chapel.

In more recent years new churches were needed in the suburbs, St. James in Green Street and St. Paul's at Tupsley were both built in the 1860's The former was destroyed by fire on December 23rd, 1901 and had to be rebuilt. Later came Holy Trinity Church at Whitecross, built in 1883 on land provided by the Custos and Vicars Choral of the Cathedral.

Early places of worship belonging to other Christian sects include the large Catholic Church of St. Francis Xavier in Broad Street, built in 1837; the Eignbrook United Reformed Church, home of the Congregationalists, originally built in 1720 but replaced in 1829 and again in 1872, and the Friends's Meeting House, up a narrow passage off King Street, which was built in 1822 although the Quakers were in Hereford as early as 1660. The Baptists were apparently late arrivals in the city - their first church, built in 1832, was recently demolished having been replaced in 1880 by a new building also in Commercial Road. The Wesleyan Church in Bridge Street, built in 1829 and refaced in 1866, and the Primitive Methodists building in Union Street are no longer used as places of worship. The former built a new church at Holmer in 1876, and the latter built churches in St. Owen Street and Chandos Street in 1880 and 1903 respectively. □

TOMB OF ST THOMAS C.1282 - A CENTRE OF PILGRIMAGE

LEFT A WATERCOLOUR BY J.M.W. TURNER OF THE CATHEDRAL AND RIVER, PAINTED IN 1795.

THE CHAINED LIBRARY IN HEREFORD CATHEDRAL

THE KING'S CASTLE

Underneath the well-cut grass of Castle Green and the adjoining Redcliffe Gardens some 1200 years of the history of Hereford lies hidden. Here, after a dry summer, the buried walls of the long-forgotten castle show as brown parched lines in the otherwise green grass. Even deeper, and only briefly seen when a sewer was laid in 1886, are the drains belonging to the castle - massive stone-walled passages in which Walter Pilley, a noted antiquarian, saw three skeletons and a pitcher jug in perfect condition.

Hereford Castle - 'one of the fairest, largest and strongest castles in England. . . in circuit nearly as large as Windsor' - was demolished after the Civil War and the grounds landscaped as a public open area in the late 17th century. We are fortunate that it still remains for it was suggested as a potential site for the County Gaol in 1795; however it was considered to be too damp and too far from the Courts, and the Gaol was eventually built in Commercial Road.

In 1809 a memorial dedicated to Lord Nelson was erected in the middle of the Green - what a pity that lack of funds meant that it had to be crowned with an urn rather than with a statue of the great man as had originally been planned.

Apart from the bowling green in the eastern part of the Green there have been no significant changes to this area of Hereford since the 18th century. The views of the cathedral and of the river remain unchanged and the Castle Pool still gives an indication of the wet moat which once completely sealed off the castle from the rest of the city.

The first castle in Hereford was probably built as a motte and bailey by Ralph, the son of the Count of Vexin, who became Earl of Hereford in about 1046 AD. The site of his castle lay close to what was then the eastern gateway into the Saxon City and the mound may still survive as Hogg's Mount at the north-eastern corner of the Green. Ralph's castle was destroyed by the Welsh in 1055 AD when they burnt the town and cathedral and took 'vast spoil and booty' back to Wales.

In 1066 William fitzOsbern, Lord of Breteuil in Normandy, was created Earl of Hereford and was doubtless responsible for the rebuilding of the castle in Hereford. He probably built the large mound to the west of Castle Green in the area which is now Redcliffe Gardens. This would then have been joined with a rampart to Hogg's Mount which, together with the existing defences of the city on the east, would have created an enclosed defended area.

Within this area, and hardly compatible with its use as a castle, were the city cemetary and St. Guthlac's monastery. The former became disused and burials were henceforth in the area around the cathedral, but St. Guthlac's monastery continued within the castle bailey until around 1144 when it was moved to a new site in Commercial Road.

The castle was forfeited to the crown in 1074 AD after Roger, William fitzOsbern's son, helped in an unsuccessful attempt to depose the King. Throughout most of the remainder of its history Hereford remained a royal castle with the sheriff being responsible for the repairs.

The castle rapidly grew in importance during the late 11th and early 12th centuries. It was beseiged in 1138, during the Wars of Succession, but held out for five weeks. In the following year it was beseiged again and finally surrendered. For a short time afterwards it was granted to Roger of Gloucester but after a rebellion it reverted to the crown.

During the latter part of the 12th and the first half of the 13th centuries the castle received almost continuous alterations. The great keep, on top of the western mound, was probably built at the beginning of the 13th century about the same time as a 'small tower' was built at a cost of £100. The castle walls were repaired in 1181-82 and a new tower was built in 1239-40 to replace one which had fallen down. Over £100 was spent on various parts of the castle between 1250 and 1252 but a survey in 1254 disclosed a great many defects. The roof of the great tower was out of repair and the steps up to it needed to be entirely rebuilt, the Jew's prison below the ring wall of the keep was unroofed, both gates needed repair and, as happened many times, the south wall of the castle was in danger of being undermined by the Wye. King John and his successor Henry III were regular visitors to Hereford and doubtless occupied the state quarters in the bailey of the castle. During the latter's reign Hereford featured prominently in the Baron's wars of the 1260's. For a time the castle was the headquarters of the Baronial party and had Peter de Montfort as its governor. It was here that Prince Edward, the eldest son of the King, having been taken prisoner at the battle of Lewes, was brought by his captor Simon de Montfort. He was permitted to exercise himself on horseback on Widemarsh Common from where, by a subterfuge, he escaped to Wigmore Castle.

A description in 1265 provides a graphic impression of the number of buildings then present in the area we now know as the Castle Green. There were the King's great hall, the King's small hall, chambers for the king and queen and their knights, the county hall, an almonry, a counting house, a stable, two gaols, a chamber for the king's clerks, an exchequer chamber, a building in which seige engines were kept, and the usual offices (kitchen, bakery, etc.). The main entrance, on the north side, led across the moat on "a great bridge of stone arches with a drawbridge in the middle".

The Edwardian conquest of Wales between 1277 and 1282 meant that Hereford Castle lost much of its importance as a royal fortress. Surveys in 1291 and 1300 indicate that the roof timbers of the great hall were beginning to decay due to the loss of lead and shingles, some 65 feet of the curtain wall had fallen, and the almonry had been demolished. Some repairs were undertaken in 1307, but when Queen Isabella, the wife of Edward II, came to Hereford in 1326 she was lodged in the Bishop's Palace, the castle being apparently in disrepair.

By 1377 the buildings were becoming ruinous and in 1387 Richard II granted the rights of pasture and herbage in the castle to Roger Ploughfield. Repairs costing almost £100 and 351 oak trees from Haywood forest arrested some of the decay at the beginning of the 15th century but when Leland visited the city in the early 16th century he noted that the whole castle was 'tending toward ruin' and that the main drawbridge was 'cleane downe'. Many of the buildings in the bailey had been demolished - he only mentions a couple of houses, a chapel and a mill.

The castle was badly damaged during the Civil War and the Surveyor General's report of 1652 gives an accurate picture of the ruinous state of the buildings and fortifications. The whole bailey area together with the Governor's Lodge (now Castle Cliffe) was only worth £6-10s per annum. The materials of the keep were worth £40 and the other buildings £20.

The castle was bought by Sir Richard Harley and several friends from John Birch in 1647 for "publique use and benefitt" and was gradually dismantled, much of the stone being used to rebuild the hall of the College of the Vicars Choral and the City Tolsey.

The landscaping followed in the latter part of the 17th century and the great mound was removed to provide gravel for the city roads. In 1873 the Green was leased to the City council for a period of 200 years. They are still responsible for its maintenance as a public open space 'for the advantage of the countie of Hereford and the inhabitants thereof.' □

HEREFORDS DEFENCES

It is now some 20 years since the City Walls Ring Road was built. Following the line of the city ditch, the construction of this road exposed the remaining parts of the City Wall for the first time for many generations. The eroded stonework looks as though the wall has been in use since the foundation of the city but it is in fact the latest of a series of defensive works which protected the city from incursions from the Welsh.

The earliest defence, only determined on the western side of the city between Victoria Street and Berrington Street, was a ditch with an internal gravel embankment, probably with a fence on top, which was constructed in the middle of the 9th century. It probably enclosed no more than half-a-dozen streets and the Cathedral precints, leaving St. Guthlac's Monastery and the city cemetery totally exposed on the east.

About AD 900 the defences were totally re-built and extended to include St. Guthlac's. The new work was well constructed and designed to look impressive from the outside. A series of vertical posts, 1m apart, were placed in post-holes on the inside of the ditch. Behind them layers of turves were laid to form a rampart. Between the embankment and the posts, split logs were placed horizontally on top of each other. The resultant face would have been about 4m high including the breast work, and a re-built section at the rear of St. Owen's Court shows how impregnable this would have been.

Timber defences such as these would only have had a limited life span and eventually the whole circuit was improved with the addition of a stone wall in front of the timber face. It was probably about 2.5m high and 2m wide with the timber breast work continuing above. The top of the rampart would have been used as a fighting platform and, for ease of access, a road some 2m wide was built inside the embankment. This first stone defence of Hereford was probably built during the first half of the 10th century, possibly to impress the Welsh princes when they met Athelstan about AD 930.

The defences of Hereford fell into disuse during the latter part of the 10th century and although they were repaired by Earl Harold in 1055, after the Welsh burnt the city and cathedral, the works were probably minor. After the Norman Conquest the city continued to grow to the north and the Saxon defences were abandoned behind the shops and houses which fronted the south side of William fitzOsbern's new market place in High Town.

The narrow alley-ways such as Church Street (Capuchin Lane) and the Booth Hall passage reflect the first attempts to cross the disused embankment, for previously the only northern gate had been at the top of Broad Street.

Richard I's charter, 800 years ago, made the citizens responsible for their own defence by fortifying the town. This they did by reusing the old defences on the east and west of the city and by constructing a new embankment and ditch around the new market place and the houses and shops in the suburbs. The new defence, crowned with a fence of bushwood and thorn palings, may also have had internal timber watch-towers. South of the river, the bridge-head settlement of St. Martin's was also protected by a similar embankment and ditch which still stands over 2m high as it crosses Bishop's Meadow.

The inadequacy of Hereford's defences against the increasing ferocity of the Welsh attacks let to the first grant of murage in AD 1224. The whole circuit took over 40 years to complete despite mandates by the King and incursions by Llewelyn

THE CITY WALL AND HALF-ROUND BASTION TOWER IN VICTORIA STREET.

THE RECONSTRUCTED LATE 9TH CENTURY DEFENSIVE TIMBER WALL WITH THE EARLY 10TH CENTURY STONE WALL IN FRONT. IN THE FOREGROUND IS PART OF THE 13TH CENTURY CITY WALL.

BELOW
BYE STREET GATE FROM THE OUTSIDE IN THE LATE 18TH CENTURY.

into the Herefordshire lowlands. When complete, Hereford was as strong a walled town as any in England. With its 17 semi-circular towers (of which two remain) and six gates, the wall enclosed an area of 38 hectares and was 1645m long.

The entrances into the city - Wye Bridge Gate, Friars' Gate, Eign Gate, Widemarsh Gate, Bye Street Gate and St. Owen's Gate—were large and impressive structures where tolls were gathered. Bye Street Gate (now lost under Commercial Square), also included the City Gaol, and part of the gatehouse adjoining Widemarsh Gate still survives as the Farmer's Club. It is here that a small gate in the wall was made by Thomas Church, a dyer, in 1582 to allow him to wash his coloured cloth in the ditch! The doorway with Thomas Church's initials can still be seen.

The gates, having last been used during the Civil War, were all demolished in the late 18th century by order of the Improvement Commissioners 'for the better accomodation of the public'. With the gates gone there was little public feeling for the walls and they gradually disappeared behind warehouses and stables built over the infilled ditch. The few remains which survive give only a pale impression of one of the most complex and strongly defended cities in the country.

The City Charters

Hereford's charters run in an unbroken sequence of almost 800 years from 1189 to 1974. The earliest extant charter, granted by Richard the First gave Hereford the rights and responsibilities which were to develop into full status as an incorporated borough. The most recent charter, granted by Elizabeth the Second, confirmed Hereford's status as a city, a title of which it is justly proud.

The process of granting a charter usually originated with the city, which petitioned the sovereign for the privileges which it most needed at that time. Not every charter gave something new; many of the charters are simply confirmations of the grants made by preceeding sovereigns, an insurance against later alteration or interference by the crown.

Many of the early charters are concerned with trade and reflect Hereford's position as the centre of a rich agricultural area, with a prosperous community of merchants and craftsmen. Their most pressing need was for a Merchant Guild, whose members could regulate business within the city, denying trading rights to outsiders, and this was granted by King John in his charter of 1215. This charter has not survived, but it was confirmed by John's son, Henry the Third, whose own charter of 1227 granted the citizens another element vital to medieval trade, in the form of a three day fair held in October.

Another preoccupation of the medieval citizens was with defence, for the city stood on the Marches of an often hostile Wales and raids across the border were an ever present hazard. In 1298 the conqueror of Wales, Edward the First, granted them the right for five years to levy tolls on certain trade goods coming in to Hereford, in order to finance the rebuilding of the city walls. A hundred years later a charter of Richard the Second allowed a similar system of tolls to pay for the rebuilding of the Wye Bridge, a vital link in the city's communications with the South, after it had been destroyed by floods. On this occasion the King also gave some practical help by giving the city thirty oak trees from his royal forest of Haywood, as well as stone from the quarries there, to use in the repairs.

At about the same time difficulties of trade and the still more difficult Welsh came together in another charter. Many Hereford merchants travelling in Wales had found themselves illegally arrested for debt contrary to their earlier charter rights, in cases where they were neither the surety nor principal debtor. They were now afraid to venture over the border and their very lucrative trade in the principality was almost at a stand-still. Accordingly in 1394 they sought and won the right to arrest any Welshman found in Hereford in retaliation for any citizen of theirs imprisoned in Wales, and to hold him until full reparation was made.

Also under Richard the Second came a grant which has a most important effect today, when the charter of 1383 established that the chief bailiff of the city should be given the more honorific title of mayor.

Another important privilege which the city obtained by charter was the right to hold property and to let it out for rent. First in 1393 came a licence to acquire a house from a certain Thomas Chippenham to use for meetings of the council and courts. This building became known as the Boothall, and part of it still survives in High Town today. The process was repeated in   ▷

SEAL FROM THE WILLIAM AND MARY CHARTER.
1690

▷ 1536 under Henry the Eighth when a wealthy and generous tailor called Richard Phelipes, several times mayor of Hereford, decided to give his city a considerable endowment of houses and land. The rent of these properties raised so much income that the city was able to lower its market tolls, giving a welcome boost to its trade.

The charters reached their peak in that granted by Elizabeth the First in 1597, under which Hereford was incorporated by the name of the mayor, aldermen and commonalty, and gained the rights of an incorporated borough. Many of the modern features of the city are there set out formally for the first time, including the offices of chief steward, town clerk and serjeants at mace. The charter also confirmed many earlier grants including the right to a Guild Merchant, three weekly markets, and two annual fairs.

Under the early Stuarts the city continued on the course set by Elizabeth, and it was left for Charles the Second to strike a blow at the city's freedom. In a move away from democracy towards a more autocratic government the King called in Hereford's charter, along with many others, and in regranting it reserved to himself the right to remove any members of the council who did not meet with his approval. This attempt at royal interference was fortunately short lived, and the charter of William the Third in 1697 restored to Hereford all its ancient rights.

At first sight the appearance of the charters is remarkably varied, ranging from Richard's simple parchment measuring 5½ x 4½ inches, to the four closely written sheets of 1597, each nearly 3 ft. square. All are written in Latin until the nineteenth century, and on further inspection other similarities in their make-up emerge.

All the charters were written on parchment (sheepskin) or vellum (calfskin), using an iron gall ink whose darkness varies with the amount of acid added to it. Coloured ink, where necessary, came from a variety of natural sources including cuttlefish, plant extracts, insects and shells. The charters were written out by clerks from the chancery office, and authenticated by the great seal attached to them with coloured tags or cords. A new seal is made for each sovereign, and ever since the Conquest it has traditionally shown the sovereign on one side enthroned, the source of justice and power, and on the other armed and mounted, ready to defend the realm against its enemies. The seals were made of beeswax in various colours, natural, white, black or green; wax is brittle and many of the seals have been lost, but many fine examples still remain, expecially on the charters of Edward the First and William and Mary.

The early charters are plain and simple, but from the sixteenth century they become ever more decorative, with initial letters enclosing portraits of the sovereign, and richly ornamented borders. The charter of Henry the Eighth shows the young king holding the orb and sceptre, all in gold leaf, while the charter of incorporation has a richly coloured portrait of Elizabeth the First enthroned in splendour in her robes of state. Such decoration was usually added at the petitioner's request, and the borders of this charter must surely have been filled in partly to the city's own specification, with their colourful flowers, birds and insects joined to coats of arms including those of Hereford itself. Later parchment came ready engraved with the sovereign's portrait, but although the result is fine and clear, it has none of the immediacy, the sense of reaching out to us across the centuries, which comes so strongly from the personal, hand-drawn decoration of the earlier charters. □

THE CHARTER OF ELIZABETH I 1597

HIDDEN BUILDINGS

Until the latter part of the 17th century, Hereford was a town of timber-framed buildings with stone only being used for churches and the more important public buildings. Many of these early timber buildings have been demolished to make way for larger 19th century shops, but several have been hidden behind new brick facades which were added in the 18th and 19th centuries to 'modernise' the older buildings. The remains of these older buildings provide a fascinating insight into how our forefathers lived in the medieval city. The oldest and one of the most interesting of our hidden timber-framed heritage is the great hall of the Bishops Palace built in the late 12th century by Bishop William de Vere within a year or two of the granting of the city's first charter. Now totally obscured by later brickwork, the remains are those of one of the most important medieval secular buildings remaining in England. In its original state it was a four-bay aisled hall with a side porch and an end chamber-block. The hall, 55 feet wide and 100 feet long and open to the roof, must have been an imposiing structure in its original state, a fit building in which the Bishop could entertain the King and his retinue during their regular visits to the city. Alterations by Bishop Bisse (1713-21) and his successors have left a mere fragment of this once magnificent hall but some of the piers, with their colonettes and scalloped capitals and part of the arch-braced roof with nail head ornamentation, still survive.

The Cathedral Close was originally surrounded by the large houses of the clergy and one of these survives, although again hidden by later brick walls. This is now 20 Church Street, the home of several of the Cathedral organists until 1930 when it was purchased by the Conservative Association. The original building, erected about 1400 AD, was a three-bay first-floor hall with a crown-post roof (which is almost complete, although hidden by later plaster ceilings) and an undercroft. Recent clearance has exposed the original ogee-headed doorway and a well-preserved timber window of four cusped ogee-arched headed lights.

The Cathedral Close has yet another timber-framed building of great antiquity. From the outside, the barn in the northeastern corner of the Close does not look as though it is of any great interest but a detailed investigation has shown that it was built in the 13th century, possibly with aisles and a scissor-braced roof. It was re-roofed in the 16th century and it was probably then that the south wall was underbuilt in stone. The earliest parts of this barn represent the second oldest of the surviving timber-framed building in Hereford.

A narrow passage between nos. 40 and 41 Bridge Street leads to a pair of timber-framed buildings. On the left is the jettied side wall of a 16th century building with a moulded bressumer and curved brackets, but the small independent building on the right was built in the last quarter of the 14th century. It was probably a cross-wing of a hall to the south which has long since disappeared. The cusped braces and the carved quatrefoil doorhead indicate the considerable ornamentation which would have been associated with a building of this period.

PART OF THE ROOF OF THE LATE 12TH CENTURY BISHOP'S PALACE

13TH CENTURY BARN IN THE CATHEDRAL CLOSE.

TIMBER FRAMING OF THE LATE 14TH CENTURY BUILDING, 41, BRIDGE STREET.

Apart from the 17th century Old House, the only visible timber-framed building in the High Town area is a small fragment of what was no. 3 High Street now perched on a shelf in the front elevation of Littlewoods Stores. When the store was being built, this 16th century building was moved on wheels into High Town and returned to its present position where, although totally inaccessible, it provides a flavour of the elaborate decoration used on these high but narrow buildings.

A little further along the south side of High Town are two more timber-framed buildings, now fronted in brick. No. 27, which has recently been restored, includes the substantial remains of a 17th century double-jettied building which has been well exposed at 1st and 2nd floor levels. Next door, in No. 26, the 1st floor ceiling of a late 16th century merchant's house can be seen from the shop. On the floor above were the bed-chambers, with the servants quarters in the attic space.

Commercial Street has two buildings of note. On the northern side, Chadd's menswear shop in no. 25 includes a series of buildings dating back to the late 15th century. They originally opened onto the western side passage, but were gradually included into the main shop. The low, heavily-,moulded ceiling beams of this shop are typical of buildings of this period. On the opposite side of the street the roof and upper part of a small 15th century hall, complete with cusped and decorated wind braces and trefoil-headed panels, has just been discovered and exposed in no. 50a.

The Booth Hall, hidden away down a side passage on the southern side of High Town, is an important example of early 15th century work. The roof has alternate tie-beam and hammer-beam trusses, the latter terminating in half figures. There are ranges of open trefoil-headed panels and the cusped windbraces form arches in the lower parts of the roof, and quatrefoils above.

Although later in date, the elaborately decorated 17th century plaster ceilings in the Conservative Club and 24 Church Street are noteworthy, whilst the slightly earlier and plainer ceiling in the first floor of the Black Lion Inn in Bridge Street is complemented by a series of wall paintings of mid 16th century date depicting the breaking of the ten commandments. Buildings often continue below the ground and the cellars can be of great interest and much older than the superstructure. Orginally designed for use as shops or meeting rooms, they are now often abandoned and forgotten. The most noteable examples are those underneath 3-7 Widemarsh Street which are of late 15th century date with fine stonework and stone vaults.

The two-centred arched doorways with moulded jambs and the carved panels let into the vault, and a later immense stone fireplace makes these underground rooms of considerable visual importance. Similar cellars, but without the decorative features, exist under several of the shops on the south side of High Town.

The hidden buildings of Hereford provide a fascinating insight into the development of the city and the way in which its inhabitants lived since its first charter was granted in 1189.

High Town

The creation of a new market place to the north of the Saxon defences after the Norman Conquest was the first step in transferring the commercial heart of the city from the Saxon ▽

THE MARKET HALL BY CLAYTON, C. 1860 PROPOSED RECONSTRUCTION.

'burh' to the new Norman suburb. At each end of the main market place a new church was founded—St. Peter's to the east end was built by Walter de Lacy before 1085, whilst All Saints (outside the old North Gate) was probably founded by William fitzOsbern for his French burgesses who settled nearby.

The large triangular market place - which probably extended westwards towards Eign Gate (with an open space between Eign Gate Street and Bewell Street), and north-eastwards to include the land between Union Street and Commercial Street - was one of the largest in the country and gives some indication of the importance attached to Hereford in the 11th and 12th centuries.

Gradually, the market stalls became more permanent structures and rows of timber-framed shops with dwellings above filled most of the area. In parts they remain, but those in the High Town area were gradually demolished in the early years of the 19th century leaving the Old House (built 1621) as an isolated reminder of Cooken Row and the Butchery.

Cooken Row, which was separated from the Old House by a narrow passage called Golden Alley, was in the central part of High Town. Here the bakers and confectioners plied their trade with the Catherine Wheel Inn at the centre. These buildings were the first to be demolished in the latter part of the 18th century.

The Butchery was a row of timber-framed buildings which was attached to the south-eastern side of the Old House and ran down the middle of St. Peter's Street towards St. Peter's Square. Part of the row was de- ▷

THE MARKET HALL IN 1856 BY W.W. GILL

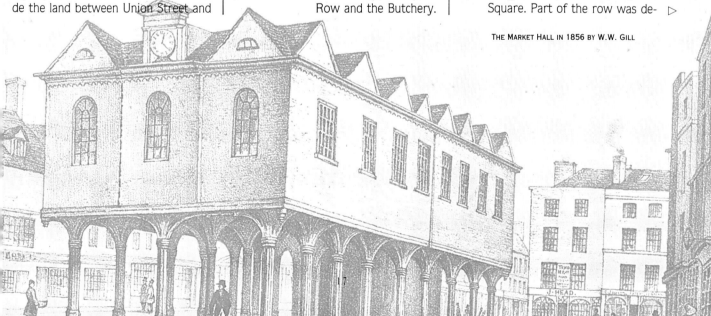

St Owen's Street Hereford

▷ molished in 1818 but the buildings adjoining the Old House, including the Old George Inn which spent its declining years as a butcher's shop, survived a little longer. Finally compensation was agreed and the buildings were demolished in 1837 leaving the Old House isolated.

The Old House continued in use as a saddlers until 1872 when Matthew Oatfield's hardware business moved in. In 1882 it was bought by the Worcester City and County Banking Company, later absorbed by Lloyd's Bank who gave the building to the city in 1928 having built a new banking chamber on the north side of High Town.

The western part of High Town contained one of the most important and impressive buildings in the city - the Old Market Hall - sadly demolished in 1862, although its position and size can be appreciated by coloured paving blocks. It was 35 feet wide and 85 feet long standing on a raised stone-flagged floor two steps high.

It was built in the latter part of the 16th century and was originally three stories high with an open-columned ground floor for the market. On the first floor was the magistrates chambers and the assize court, with the City Guilds (fourteen in all including bakers, barbers, butchers, clothiers, coopers, glovers, tanners and weavers) using the second storey. At the end of the 18th century the top floor was deemed unsafe and the building was reduced to a two storey edifice. This was stuccoed, thus losing much of its elevational splendour, and although plans were prepared for its restoration these came to naught and the building was finally demolished - the material being sold to William Davies of Widemarsh Street for £200.

Four of the pillars of the market hall still survive at Holmer Hall where they now support a summer house, and the quarter-jacks and bells belonging to the clock are in the City Museum. High Town also contained the High Cross, and the Tolsey, used for Council

Meetings and the payment of tolls, which was demolished in 1768. At earlier times it probably included the Bull Ring, used for bull fights, and the pillory and stocks.

St. Peter's Square was the eastern extremity of the market place and also contained many more buildings than it now possesses. St. Peter's Church was almost hidden by buildings on the south and east making Union Street a narrow passage. The Shire Hall, built in 1819, replaced the County Goal which was moved into a new building in Commercial Road. The large open areas of High Town and St. Peter's Square are in size very much as they were originally designed but the loss of the many 16th century timber-framed buildings and especially the Market Hall, is deplorable.

☐

ABOVE.
BUTCHERS ROW 1815, BY DAVID COX, ON SHOW AT CHURCHILL GARDENS MUSEUM

ROYALIST *Hereford in* the CIVIL WAR

Hereford , the King's stronghold, was unprepared when the Parliamentary Army, under the Earl of Stamford, appeared at the Gates of the City on 30th September, 1642. Although there were about 300 soldiers inside the walls, the defences were in disrepair, and the powder magazine was nearly empty. The Royalists fled, and the City was taken.

Lord Stamford, with 1,000 troopers on foot, and Sir Robert Harley, with 100 horse, took possession and plundered the terrified City. After only eight weeks, the Roundheads left for Gloucester, as they had no "money, credit, bread or provender".

On their return, the Royalists, with Sir Richard Cave in charge, had to face another attack on 25th July, 1643 led by General Waller. An entry in the Baptismal Register of St. Peter's Church confirms the date. It reads -

"Edward Jones, ye sonne of Edward Jones and Elizabeth, his wife, was borne ye 23rd April, 1643, and was baptised ye 25th of July, ye same month which day came to ye City of Hereford Sir William Waller".

Cave had no choice but to surrender and agree to terms which included a ransom of £3,000. Waller then levied heavy fines upon the citizens in lieu of plunder, however, he soon left the City with his men in order to re-provision. The demoralised city was revitalised by Colonel Barnabas Scudamore who worked hard on the defences with the citizens of Hereford over the next two years, knowing full well that the

Parliamentarians would be back in strength.

A wanderfully detailed picture of life in the city is given to us in the account books of Mrs. Joyce Jeffries of Widemarsh Street, kept from 1638 to 1647. She records payment towards the repair of the defences, help with the expense of billeting soldiers, and she even had her house burned down in the scorched earth clearances of the suburbs. The orchards gardens and trees outside the City were all destroyed in the expectation of a siege.

Joyce Jeffries, however, had arranged for her window glass to be carefully removed and buried in two large chests in the garden. Six months later she paid David Williams 6d. to dig them up again !

About 4,000 people waited in trepidation inside the walled City assisting the 1,500 soldiers in preparation for War. On 31st July, 1645, Lord Leven and the Scottish Army of some 14,000 troops surrounded the City and demanded its surrender from Colonel Scudamore. He replied,

"My Lord, I am not to give up the King's Garrison upon any summons or letter; neither shall it be in the power of the Mayor or other to condescend to any such proposition made unto him. I was set here by the King's command and I shall not quit it, but by special order from His Majesty or the Prince, and with this resolution I shall persist in Hereford"

THIS LAST OF JULY 1645
(SIGNED) BARNABAS SCUDAMORE.

Five weeks of siege and assault and still the City held out, in spite of the destruction of an arch of the Wye Bridge and the Churches of St. Martin and St. Owen: even the Chapter House roof was stripped of lead for shot

Finally, King Charles, with 3,000 horse, was reported to be travelling towards Hereford from Worcester, Lord Leven and the Scottish Army retreated swiftly, and on 4th September, King Charles I entered the City, saved through the loyalty and gallantry of his supporters. Barnabas Scud-

LETTER FROM KING CHARLES I TO PRINCE RUPERT SENDING ASSISTANCE TO THE CITY.

amore was immediately knighted, with two of his Officers and the King gave the City a new Coat of Arms and the right to use the Motto "Invictae fidelitatis praemium" - The Reward of Invincible Loyalty.

The Siege of Hereford is still remembered today when we look at the City's Coat of Arms. The ten silver saltires or crosses, depict the Scottish Army encircling the City and the buckles on the collars of the supporters are taken from the arms of Lord Leven.

Jubilation at the relief of the City turned to sorrow and acute deprivation when Hereford was captured by a dramatic Parliamentary ruse, led by Colonel John Birch at 6 o'clock on the morning of the 18th December, 1645.

Six Roundheads, dressed as labourers, hid in a vegatable cart and were driven through the snow towards Bysters Gate.   ▷

ABOVE

'ROARING MEG' MADE AND USED AT THE SIEGE OF GOODRICH CASTLE. NOW AT CHURCHILL GARDENS MUSEUM. THE LONGEST CIVIL WAR MORTAR EXTANT.

The drawbridge was lowered and they swiftly overpowered the guards. Without an alarm raised, one hundred and fifty men rushed down from their hiding place in the ruins of St. Guthlac Priory - where the Bus Station is today - followed by other troops hidden in the woods on Aylestone Hill. The gates swung fully open and the City was occupied without a struggle.

The captors siezed eleven pieces of ordnance, forty barrels of powder and £40,000 worth of money and plate. Colonel Birch was rewarded for his actions by a Parliamentary Grant of £6,000 and the Governorship of the City; he quartered himself in the Bishop's Palace and marshal law commenced.

The Cathedral, nearby, suffered the removal of about 170 brasses "by sacriligious hands" to be melted down as "old metal" together with damage to monuments. Dean Croft, in his pulpit, preached strongly against the sacrilage, ignoring his personal danger. Colonel Birch stepped in to prevent his shooting by a squad of musqueteers. However, the Dean and Canons were ejected from their homes and the City was held in the grip of Parliamentary Committees and reduced to penury until the Restoration in 1660.

Hereford changed hands four times in the Civil War until permanently occupied by Parliament. Five Governors held it for the King, two were captured, two were killed sword in hand, and when Birch arrived in the City, the last Royalist Governor, Barnabas Scudamore, escaped across the frozen River Wye heading for Ludlow, and lived to fight another day. ☐

LADY ALICE LINGEN

SIT HENRY LINGEN, WHO HELD GOODRICHCASTLE FOR THE KING. HE LATER BECAME M.P. FOR HEREFORD. HIS PORTRAIT CAN BE SEEN IN THE OLD HOUSE. ARTIST UNKNOWN. C. 1640

The Changing Face of Hereford

Unlike many other towns and cities, Hereford suffered relatively little during the craze for redevelopment in the 1960's and early 1970's. It is true that several important buildings were lost, to be replaced by mediocre modern structures which have damaged part of the streetscape, but nevertheless most of the architectural character of the central part of the city dates from the 18th and 19th centuries.

In 1725 Defoe described Hereford as being 'mean built and very dirty'; the city had suffered economic decline and lagged

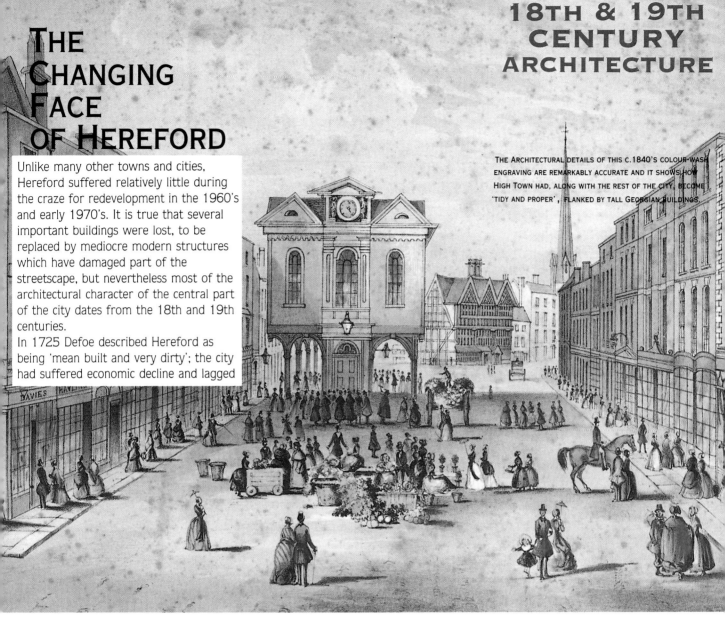

THE ARCHITECTURAL DETAILS OF THIS C.1840'S COLOUR-WASH ENGRAVING ARE REMARKABLY ACCURATE AND IT SHOWS HOW HIGH TOWN HAD, ALONG WITH THE REST OF THE CITY, BECOME 'TIDY AND PROPER', FLANKED BY TALL GEORGIAN BUILDINGS.

behind the rest of the country in architectural taste. But in 1697 Dr. Brewster had built the first fashionable brick house in Widemarsh Street, the Mansion House, and this was followed by an increasing number of others so that by 1833 the city was described as 'tidy and proper'.

The old timber-framed buildings, now out of fashion, were replaced by new brick ones or hidden behind brick facades. At the very least their ornate carved timbers were hidden by plaster. Even the Market Hall that once stood in the middle of High Town was 'modernised' in 1792. The new demand for symmetrical facades and large windows with balanced sashes evolved into the elegant Georgian style, the British architectural response to the Italian Renaissance. This lasted from the start of the 18th century until the early decades of the 19th century, and its influence is still felt today.

Many of these fine town houses survive, though few are lived in, and in many

cases the muted natural texture and colour of the local bricks have been covered by layers of paint and render. St. Owen Street and Bridge Street have particularly good examples of early 18th century houses, whilst late 18th century examples can be seen in High Town, St. John's Street and St. Martin's Street. Without actually venturing inside, or around the backs of these houses it is difficult to see which are complete buildings and which are merely facades added to older timber frames. To compound the difficulty, several structures, such as Barclay's Bank in Broad Street, were completely rebuilt behind their Georgian facades during this century. In the early 19th century there was a short-lived fashion for stuccoed facades, with the bricks rendered and lined to imitate stone. Another feature of this period is the iron balcony added at first floor level: there are examples of these in Castle Street and Widemarsh Street. From the end of the 18th century onwards the city streets were opened up, thus

losing some of their medieval character, especially after the Paving Licencing and Lighting Act of 1774. The demolition of the ancient city gates between 1782 and 1798 was designed to increase the air flow within the walls and to provide better entrances to the city itself. Norgate, to the south of All Saints Church, was widened to make it into a continuation of Broad Street. Similar plans to widen Church Street were not, fortunately, carried out and it retains much of the flavour and character of a medieval town street.

In High Town, the large Norman market place had been colonised over the years by timber-framed buildings, most of which were pulled down by 1837. The magnificent Market Hall was demolished in 1862, leaving once again a wide open space which was by then flanked by 18th and 19th century facades. The architecture of the 19th century was characterised by the adaptation of many

▷

THE OLD NARROW NORGATE WAS OPENED UP AT THE END OF THE 18TH CENTURY TO BECOME A CONTINUATION OF BROAD STREET, CREATED ONE OF THE BEST STREETSCAPES IN THE CITY.

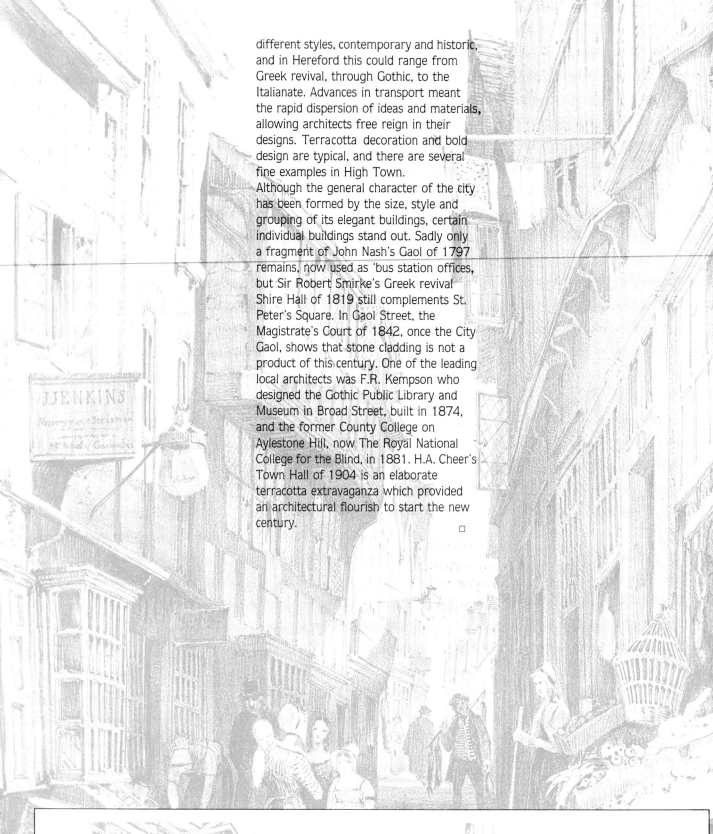

different styles, contemporary and historic, and in Hereford this could range from Greek revival, through Gothic, to the Italianate. Advances in transport meant the rapid dispersion of ideas and materials, allowing architects free reign in their designs. Terracotta decoration and bold design are typical, and there are several fine examples in High Town.

Although the general character of the city has been formed by the size, style and grouping of its elegant buildings, certain individual buildings stand out. Sadly only a fragment of John Nash's Gaol of 1797 remains, now used as 'bus station offices, but Sir Robert Smirke's Greek revival Shire Hall of 1819 still complements St. Peter's Square. In Gaol Street, the Magistrate's Court of 1842, once the City Gaol, shows that stone cladding is not a product of this century. One of the leading local architects was F.R. Kempson who designed the Gothic Public Library and Museum in Broad Street, built in 1874, and the former County College on Aylestone Hill, now The Royal National College for the Blind, in 1881. H.A. Cheer's Town Hall of 1904 is an elaborate terracotta extravaganza which provided an architectural flourish to start the new century. □

The Green Dragon

BROAD STREET · HEREFORD · HR4 9BG 0432 - 272506

A HOTEL OF DISTINCTION . . . . a visitor to Hereford who strolls along Broad Street in the quiet of the evening and gazes suddenly skywards, might well be surprised to find himself being looked down upon by a large, green, fire-breathing dragon.

For many centuries now, an inn of some description has stood on the site of the latter-day building. Today it combines all the comforts of a first class contemporary hotel, with a keen pervading sense of the historic.

 Trusthouse Forte

INDUSTRY

Traditionally, Hereford's industries have been associated directly or indirectly with local agriculture. The earliest industrial features to be identified in the city are a pair of late 7th century corn drying ovens found during excavations in 1967. Cornmilling was clearly an important industry by medieval times and was dominated by the clergy. In 1988 the City's Archaeology Unit located the probable remains of a medieval water mill at Monkmoor, once owned by St. Guthlac's monastery; this excavation took place due to the generosity of the developers, Morbaine Ltd. There were two corn mills on the Wye in the early 16th century, as well as others using the water flow in the City Ditch and of the Eign Brook. The two corn mills on the Wye were destroyed by order of Henry VIII to improve navigation, along with two fulling mills connected with the wool and cloth industry. This was, up until the Reformation, one of the city's staple industries using Welsh cloth sold in the Booth Hall. Caps were also made in the city up to the 16th century.

Hides from local cattle were used in several local trades, notably in glove making. Several tanneries were established, and by the early 18th century the former Monkmoor corn mill had been converted into a leather mill. Later still this was expanded into a large industrial concern owned by Herron's of London, treating sheepskins, wool and leather. There were other large tanneries in Widemarsh Street and in Barton Road by the 18th century.

Hereford is, of course, world renowned for its cider, using the apples from the many thousands of acres of local orchards. But other local products, hops and barley, could also be made into that alternative and delightful alcoholic beverage - beer. Up until the last century most breweries in the City were small enterprises attached to public houses, but several of these increased output and produced a surplus. The biggest brewery, owned by Watkins & Sons, moved to Bewell Street by 1845 and was greatly expanded in 1872. The 'Hereford Brewery' was noted for its 'Old Hereford Ale', 'Watkins Cream Stout' and especially, its 'Golden Sunlight Ale.'

Agriculture also created a demand for products, particularly farm machinery. Naylor's, one of the largest firms in this field, was founded in the 1860's and by the early 1900's were specialising in oil engines as well. Harding Brothers were another large firm specialising both in ironfounding and ironmongery. An earlier iron foundry had been started in 1827 by Captain Radford, who was also involved with local shipbuilding. He built a new works on Friars Street along with a terrace of cottages for his workers. However, the venture was not a success and the works were taken over by Watkins & Sons and converted to a steam powered flour mill. Later in the century the Watkins Imperial Mills were the first buildings in Hereford to be lit by electricity. The original foundry buildings still remain, although much altered. ▷

GOLDEN SUNLIGHT

Keep the Golden Sunlight in your house it is a light pale Golden Ale. of pleasant flavour & wonderful value. it is good, it is light it is pure you will

like it better than the stronger Burton Ale and it will not disagree with you

Charles Watkins & Son The Hereford Brewery (Established 1834)

PALE ALE

COMPARE IT WITH OTHER BEERS. "– MATCHED WITH MINE ARE AS MOONLIGHT UNTO SUNLIGHT, AND AS WATER UNTO WINE " Tennyson.

23

LEFT

THE LEATHER MILL, MONKMOOR ON BUCKS. C. 1732 PROSPECT OF HEREFORD VIEWED FROM AYLESTONE HILL.

▷ Other notable industrial buildings still survive including the steam flour mill in Bath Street built by the Rev. John Venn's Society for Aiding the Industrious in 1848, and, tucked away in Gwynne Street, a fine, five-storey warehouse built in polychrome brick. This warehouse, built in the late 19th century, was added to a series of buildings owned by Rogers & Co., one of the largest corn-factors in the area, whose main offices fronted Bridge Street. At the Broomy Hill waterworks to the west of the city the fine Italianate tower, 101 foot high, dates from 1882.

Until the present century, Hereford's only large scale manufacturing industry was the tile industry. Good quality local clays had been exploited for brick and tile manufacture for centuries on a relatively small scale, but in the 1840's the Albert Steam Pipe, Tile, Pottery, Building and Artistic Brick Company set up a large works at Holmer which specialised in art facing and ornamental brick as well as terracotta. Later, Godwin's, who had set up a decorative tile works at Lugwardine, were also established at Holmer and in 1884 built the larger Victoria Tile Works off College Road between the railway and disused canal. They exported their enamelled, embossed and hand-painted tiles all over the world, and these are now collector's items. ☐

GRAIN WAREHOUSE IN GWYNNE STREET.

THE WYE NAVIGATION

After the Romans left Britain, their roads fell into disrepair and for over a thousand years even the best stretches of the King's highway were little more than mud tracks, badly rutted in the dry summer months and impassable quagmires in wet winters. Little wonder, then, that merchants sent their heavier goods by water. The Wye was probably navigable from the Bristol Channel to Hereford, some 69 miles, before the Norman conquest and there is a reference to a wharf near the Castle as early as 1256. It was not an easy river to navigate and could only be used when the water levels were sufficiently high. In addition to natural hazards, boatmen had to compete with powerful mill owners who built weirs across the river to harness the water power waterwheels. There were many attempts made to deal with these illegal obstructions, none of which were very effective An Act of 1661 allowed Sir William Sandys to improve the navigation of the Wye by removing obstructions and building locks but his scheme failed.

An Act of 1696 empowered commissioners to levy a county rate to pay for river improvements and in its preamble the 'free and open Navigation upon the Rivers Wye and Lugg, and the Streams falling into them' was stressed, clarifiying the long-established right of passage on the whole river. As this Act has never been repealed, the right of passage remains to this day. The work largely entailed the removal of weirs but this meant that the river ran unchecked and shallows were uncovered; in 1727 another Act allowed the rebuilding of some of the weirs to slow the river down and increase its depth. Barges presumably passed through these obstructions by way of flash-locks and the new improvements certainly allowed larger craft to reach Hereford and a steady trade grew up. Later in the century some 38,500 tons of cargo went downstream from the city each year, including wool, corn, meal, timber, and - of course - cider. 15,700 tons came upriver, mainly coal, but also salt, pottery, tea, glass and Coalbrookdale grates.

The growth of this trade led to other schemes to improve the navigation but it was not until 1809 that an Act was passed to allow a private company to build a towpath between Lydbrook and Hereford. Up until this time most of the shallow-keeled barges had been hauled upstream by gangs of men, bow-hauliers, usually working in teams of 10 or more. The new towpath, opened in 1811, allowed the use of horses instead.

The hey-day of Wye river traffic was undoubtedly in the early nineteenth century when barges such as the *Mayflower*, the *Eliza*, the *Hereford* and the *Thomas & Mary* loaded and unloaded their cargoes on Hereford's quays. This inland city also became a small ship-building centre using local timber to build river barges and the occasional sea-going vessel such as the 170 ton brig launched from the Bishop's Meadow in 1823. In 1829, William Radford's yard built the 31 ton paddle steamer *Paul Pry* for the short-lived Wye Steamboat Company, and a second steamer, the 27 ton *Water Witch*, in 1834. By the 1840's the industry had almost disappeared but small pleasure boats were still being made by Richard Jordan in his yard near the Wye Bridge up until the 1890's

The belated arrival of the Hereford & Gloucester Canal at Monkmoor in 1845 took away much of the river traffic and the rest disappeared after the arrival of the steam railway in Hereford in the mid-1850's. The river is now used by rowers and canoeists and remains an important part of Hereford life.

□

LOADED BARGE BOW-HAULED UPSTREAM BY A GANG OF MEN ON THE BANK IN 1778.

EDWARD DAYES' 1793 WATERCOLOUR SHOWS BARGES MOORED JUST UPSTREAM OF THE WYE BRIDGE.

The Herefordshire & Gloucestershire Canal

As early as 1777 Robert Whitworth suggested the building of two canals to link the Wye at Hereford with the Severn; one would head for the new canal town of Stourport, via Leominister, the other going via Ledbury to Gloucester. The second scheme was revived in 1789 and an Act was passed in 1791 enabling the Herefordshire & Gloucestershire Canal Company to be established. Work started at the eastern end of the line under the direction of Josiah Clowes and the canal reached Ledbury in 1798, by which time much of the initial enthusiam for the scheme had evaported.

After decades of apathy, the company appointed a young horticulturist, Stephen Ballard, as their new manager and engineer in 1827. Mainly thanks to his drive and enthusiasm work on the Hereford section finally began in 1839. The canal approached the city through a short tunnel under Aylestone Hill and ended at a large basin near to Barr's Court, Monkmoor. It was finished in 1845, by which time the Railway Mania was under way and even the usually irrepressible Ballard was worried about the 'bad prospects that

◁ surround our canal'. Transporting building materials for the new railways provided an unexpected income for the cash-starved canal, and the delays in building a rail link between Hereford and Worcester meant that a reasonable amount of trade survived until the 1860's. In 1881 the canal east of Ledbury was finally closed; within a few years the small amount of local traffic on the now isolated Hereford section had ceased and the canal basin was filled in during the 1890's. Only a few traces of the canal in the vicinity of the city survive, of an enterprise that arrived half a century too late. □

Railways

Although there had been a proposal to build a railway from Lydbrook to Hereford in 1801, the first line to the city opened in 1829, the same year as the famous Rainhill trials on the Liverpool & Manchester Railway had proved that the steam locomotive had come of age. However, the Hereford Tramroad was a horse-drawn plateway built mainly to transport coal to the city from South Wales and was effectively an extension to other lines running north from the Brecknock Canal. The well engineered route started at Monmouth Cap, ran through a 200 yard tunnel at Haywood, just south of Hereford, before approaching the city on a long, curving embankment. The terminus, which included a counting house, tram shed, weighing machine, workshop and cottages, was just to the south of the Wye Bridge, and the embankment can still be seen. The rails were 'L' shaped cast-iron plates fixed to cast-iron sleepers and laid on stone blocks.

Standard gauge steam railways were late arriving in Hereford; indeed it was the last county town in England to be

HUNDERTON BRIDGE RESTORED AS PART OF A CYCLE-TRACK AND FOOTPATH.

THE MIDDLE OF THE THREE BASINS AT THE BARR'S COURT TERMINUS SHORTLY AFTER IT OPENED IN 1845

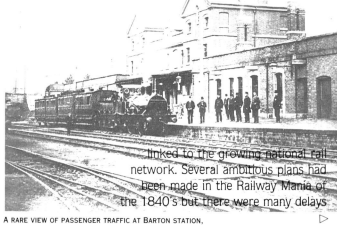

linked to the growing national rail network. Several ambitious plans had been made in the Railway Mania of the 1840's but there were many delays

A RARE VIEW OF PASSENGER TRAFFIC AT BARTON STATION, ▷

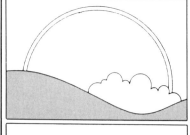

◁ before the city saw its first railway locomotive. The Shrewsbury & Hereford Railway opened for goods traffic in July 1853 but passengers wishing to travel from Hereford to Shrewsbury had to be taken by coach as far as Ludlow and it was not until the December of the following year that passenger traffic started from Barr's Court station. This opened shortly before Barton station, on the other side of the city, terminus of the Newport, Abergavenny & Hereford Railway which had acquired and closed the old Hereford Tramroad.

At the joint banquet at the Shirehall to mark of the opening of the two lines the guests were called upon to celebrate the 'nuptials of our fair and fertile county with the great world of manufacturing industry'. The railways continued to expand; the broad gauge Hereford, Ross and Gloucester Railway opened in 1855, followed in 1860 by the line to Worcester. The Great Western Railway took over most of these independent lines although it shared the line to Shrewsbury with its great rivals, the London & North Western Railway. However, the line to Brecon, which had been opened by the Hereford, Hay and Brecon Railway in stages from 1862, was taken over by the Midland Railway in 1868. The Great Western banned their trains from Barton station and until the dispute was sorted out a few years later the Midland Railway used a tempory station at Moorfields.

For many years Hereford was a busy railway centre serving its county and the adjacent parts of Wales. A tremendous amount of goods traffic went through on the vital trunk route between South Wales and the industrial North West of England and most of the larger local industries had their own sidings. Obviously, the most important local traffic was agricultural.

Following the Beeching cuts of the early 1960's the trains to Brecon and to Gloucester were closed, and railways in Hereford itself were rationalised. Barton station, which had closed to passengers as early as 1892, was finally closed completely in 1979. Barr's Court remains, and its fine station buildings are a reminder of the importance the railways once had.

☐

Roads

The lack of an adequate road network had been a continuing problem for Hereford since medieval times, although it was the poor state of the roads that delayed the arrival of the besieging Scottish Army in 1645 and might have helped to save the City. Although the main streets inside the city were dramatically improved after the Paving, Licencing and Lighting Act of 1774, in 1730 local roads nearby were described as being 'so ruinious and bad that many parts thereof are impassable', and at the start of the 19th century an irate witness to a Royal Commission on the county's roads exclaimed 'Roads! We have no roads'. The turnpike trusts

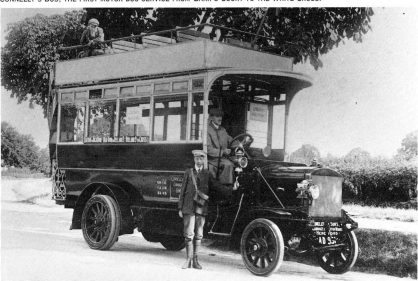

set up in the 18th century to alleviate the problem did improve the situation but even in 1853 a letter appeared in the Hereford Times complaining that the road near to Shelwick bar was 'worse athan the Bog of Athlone', The tolls on the turnpike were stopped in 1870.

Despite the state of the roads, by 1774 there was a direct stage coach service to London for those willing to undertake the uncomfortable 36 hour journey. By the 1830's, the height of the stage coach era, there were coaches to Shrewsbury, Birmingham, Bristol, Bath, Brecon, Carmarthen and Aberystwyth, and the 'Mazeppa' took only 15 hours to reach London. The principal coaching Inns were the Redstreak Tree, the New Inn, the City Arms Hotel, the Greyhound and the Green Dragon, but several other Inns were also used. Stage-coach travel suffered a severe decline

Air Transport

In 1629 the then Bishop of Hereford, Francis Godwin, published a book called 'The Man in the Moone' in which his hero is carried aloft in a swan-powered flying machine. Despite Bishop Godwin's advanced ideas on aviation the first aeroplane to land in the city did not do so until 1912, when a Bleriot monoplane landed at the Racecourse. Throughout the inter-war years there were many demonstration flights to and from the racecourse, as well as several air races, but plans to create a municipal airport on the site were postponed until after the Second World War. When this did open, in 1947, it was shortlived, closing in 1951. ☐

◁ following the arrival of railways, and had virtually disappeared by the beginning of the 1860's.

The invention of the internal combustion engine later in the century was eventually to change the character of Hereford as it did everywhere else in the world. Hereford had its won short-lived motor industry in the early 1900's when the Smooth-Geared Auto-Car Syndicate operated in Commercial Road. The first local motor-bus in the city started in 1908. ☐

ROADS AND COMMUNICATIONS, PAST AND INTO THE FUTURE

Hereford children are taught two possible sources for the name of their city, one being from the Welsh 'Henffordd' or 'Old Way' and the other from the Old English, meaning 'Army Ford'. Welsh people still use the former in their own language but the more accepted derivation describes a place where a marching column can cross a river in close order. When the place stands at one of the three main gateways to Wales, the river is the Wye and the time the early 7th century then the odds are that there will be an important military station not far away. And so there was, and it commanded the crossing of the river Wye here at Hereford for more than 800 years. The ford became a wooden bridge and stonework was added later by order of Henry I. It became pretty ruinous at times and in 1383, the year of Hereford's first Mayor, Richard II granted by charter the supply of 30 oaks and a good supply of stone 'in aid of repairs'. Until 1597 this was to be the only Wye bridge in the county whilst in 1645, during the Civil War seige, it briefly ceased to be a bridge altogether when one arch was removed to frustrate the efforts of the Scots army. For very many years it had a defended gateway, rather like that still to be seen at Monmouth, but this went in 1782. There was some widening in 1826 and although traffic engineers have often been criticised for under estimating their design figures no-one then could reasonably have dreamt of the future vast numbers of horseless carriages, more than 24,000 a day, that would be crossing the bridge just

140 years later! With the coming of the Motor Car Age the old bridge took on an entirely different order of use and by 1938, 6000 vehicles were crossing over each day, rising to over 10,000 by 1954 and to 20,000 by 1961. Some tribute to the builders of the 15th century who made what someone has described as 'this poem in stone'!

It had long been apparent that urgent relief was needed and in 1965 the dual carriageway cantilever prestressed reinforced concrete Greyfriars Bridge was built not many yards upstream in harmony with the old bridge and as further funds became available from the Ministry of Transport and County Council the city was able to set about the design and construction of the long awaited north-south and east-west relief roads and other vital trunk and country road improvements. These quite quickly led in turn towards the evolution of the 'precinct city' visualised in 1946 by George Cadbury in his 'Hereford Walls'. First came Eign gate, a pioneering scheme of 'pedestrianisation' which removed the danger, noise, fumes and visual impact of some 7,500 vehicles per day and gave the street back to the pedestrian, as well as increased profit to the shopkeeper. Church Street was repaved soon afterwards and in 1973 High Town itself was finally relieved of the daily conflict between 15,000 pedestrians struggling to negotiate the infamous 'Zebra' crossing against 9,500 often fuming motorists. The reduction in traffic flows enabled the High Street footway, as narrow as 3 foot 10 inches

in places, to be widened for the benefit of the 5,000 pedestrians a day crowding through at that time. Pedestrianisation and repaving of Commercial Street and St. Peter's Street completed the long programme in 1988 and the effects of all these schemes, the associated comprehensive developments up to the city walls and the many other improvements in the central conservation area stimulated and made possible by the introduction of the Ring Road have combined to make the centre of Hereford, for its size, one of the most attractive and buoyant in the country. Meanwhile traffic over the new bridge and along the relief road has continued to increase and saturation levels are being reached on sections of the A49 and A465 trunk roads, the relief road and the major radial connections. New measures of relief road and the major radial connections. New measures of relief to the central network are gradually taking shape as part of the new phase of expansion beyond the ring road to the north bordered by Commercial Road, Widemarsh Street and the railway. At the northern city boundary, the Roman road improvement scheme, designed long ago as an essential northern relief road, started in the late 1960's and stopped in 1972, is resuming its halting progress towards a link with the new eastern A49/A465 bypass promised for 1995.

May these new highways play their full part in paving the way for an efficient system of transportation for Hereford's entry into the 21st Century. □

The art of cider making was
established in the region
long before Hereford's
Charter was granted 800
years ago. H P Bulmer
has been making its fine
ciders in the City for
over 100 years and today
Bulmers Cider is enjoyed
around the World.

BY APPOINTMENT TO H.M. QUEEN, CIDER MAKERS
H.P. BULMER LIMITED, HEREFORD, ENGLAND

FORWARD TO THE PAST
A BRIEF LOOK AT SOCIAL HOUSING

RIGHT   VICTORIA PARK - COLLEGE, 1988
BELOW   THE GARDEN CITY - 1902

In early Britain, it was Christian or philantropic charities which took care of the needy. Housing for the poor was accomplished by various means, the most durable being the Almshouse. The history of the Almshouse can be traced back to Norman times, with their heyday occurring after the dissolution of the monasteries.

In 1066, the population of England and Wales was about two million. At the end of the seventeenth century, it was five million, with an enormous 7% growth between the years 1811 to 1821. This rapid increase in population caused major social and environmental problems at a time when corporate Local Government did not exist - it was not until 1835 that the system we would recognise today came into being.

In the eighteenth and nineteenth centuries, with transport systems making great advances, the increasingly large population became more mobile. People converged on the new industrial towns in the search for employment and factory owners responded by constructing cheap and poorly conceived housing for their new workers. The strain this placed upon the infastructure was considerable, with little or no provision being made for the supply of drinking water, for sewage disposal or for refuse collection.

Matters came to a head in 1831, with a series of devastating Cholera epidemics. These diseases forced, for the first time, the State to intervene with the living conditions of its citizens. The 1832 Cholera Act led the way for change but, regrettably, the legislation was based upon the false premise that all housing problems resulted from insanitary conditions. Because the problem had been inaccurately defined, there was little real improvement in the housing of the working classes for a further seventy years. It took a global conflict, the First World War, to act as a catalyst for real change.

The Housing and Town Planning Act, 1919, was the turning point for public housing. The legislation was intended to assist with the provision of 'homes for heroes' and to provide enough good housing for those in need. Eventually, the Government thought, private landlords would take over this function, but that objective was never achieved.

In the inter-war period, demand for housing outstripped supply, but the 1919 Act did start to redress the problem - before the legislation only 5% of housing was publicly funded; between the war years, this figure increased to 30%.

The City of Hereford has always been prepared to encourage housing initiatives and at the turn of the century, entered into a partnership with Hereford Co-operative Housing Limited to construct 85 houses on land that the Council owned. The agreement was innovative for its time, and it set the wheels in motion for the Council to embark upon the construction of Local Authority owned houses; the first dwellings being occupied in 1902.

In the last eighty years, Hereford city has built some 8,550 dwellings for sale and rent. In 1989, approximately 5,000 houses and flats are still under management, the balance having been sold to first-time buyers or the sitting tenant under various Acts of Parliament.

The 1980's have been a decade of change for public housing. In this period, the Council has been forced to develop new ways of providing affordable housing. It is, perhaps, appropriate to make a comparison between the council's earliest partnership housing scheme with its most recent; in both instances, land owned by the City has been leased to an industrial and provident society for them to provide homes for sale and rent. In 1989 the City Council is pledged to create a new non-profit making Industrial and Provident Society to continue with a building programme designed to help those in urgent need of good homes. It seems that no matter how far society progresses, you cannot stop history from repeating itself. Perhaps, with this in mind, we can predict what the next eight hundred years will bring - so let's look forward to the past!

Public Health in Hereford

Before the early nineteenth century there was no comprehensive system of local government and no central department responsible for the health of the people. At that time, cities were unhealthy places where, what was termed 'the labouring classes' lived in insanitary and over crowded conditions, lacking proper drainage or safe water supplies and often infested with bed bugs and lice. Diseases such as cholera, typhoid, typhus and diphtheria thrived in these conditions and were endemic in most cities.

In 1842, the Poor Law Commission, reported to Parliament on Sanitary Conditions of the Labouring Population of Great Britain.

This report resulted in Parliament enacting the Public Health Act 1848, enabling a General Board of Health and local boards of health empowered to appoint Inspectors of Nuisances, the fore-runner of today's Environmental Health Officer. Local Government districts were established by the Public Health Act 1872, and the foundations of today's public health laws were laid by the Public Health Act 1875. The great Victorian public health reforming movement was forging ahead with the momentum so typical of that era.

Hereford was considered a relatively healthy city by national standards at the beginning of the nineteenth century, although today we would be appalled at the conditions prevailing at that time. Water supplies were mainly drawn from wells driven into the gravel layer underlying the City at an average thickness of thirty feet. Sanitary facilities consisted mainly of privies and middens, the contents of which polluted water supplies and which were emptied into the several running streams which surrounded the City, and eventually discharged into the Wye. In 1852, a Mr. Curley, an eminent local sanitary engineer, was instructed by the Town council to report on the problem. He stated "I witnessed such scenes of filth and uncleanliness in the City as I did not believe could exist in a civilised community."

In 1855, the City Council entered into a contract for works for the drainage and sewerage of the city at an estimated cost of £25,000. The population of Hereford at that time was 12,000 and the new system, whilst greatly improving the sanitary state of the city, discharged into the Wye, to the considerable annoyance of local fishermen, one of whom being a barrister residing at Huntingdon, brought the matter before the County Court.

A new sewerage works constructed near Park Street was opened on 17th May, 1890. Seven years later, a refuse destructor capable of burning eight tons of refuse per day, was erected on the same site.

An adequate and potable water supply is an essential requisite to any healthy community, a fact recognised and industriously pursued by the Victorian authorities. Hereford City Waterworks were commenced in October 1856, and were improved and extended on several occasions.

On 10th November, 1873, the City Council formed a Sanitary Committee, which immediately appointed Dr. Vavasour Sandford, Medical Officer of Health, a part-time appointment. An Inspector of Nuisances was also appointed and began work on improving the public health of the city. The first report to the Committee dealt with over forty cottages which lacked water, drainage or other sanitary accommodation, and were, therefore, unfit for human habitation. Such was the industry employed by the Committee and its officers, that by 1910 the then Medical Officer of Health, Dr. Miller, reported that the death rate was the lowest ever recorded in the City.

The Sanitary and foods and Drugs Inspector, Mr. Prothero, was described as the eyes, ears and nose of the Medical Officer of Health. It was his duty to inspect the City for nuisances, to overlook the drainage, water closets and privies. he had to see to the inside and outside of all dwelling houses. even to smokey chimneys, defective windows, dilapidated pantries, dangerous cellar windows and ill-paved back yards. He also ensured that food sold within the city was fit to eat. In 1909, he issued 470 notices of warning concerning nuisances, 410 of which were complied with at once. In three cases legal proceeding ensued.

As public health in Hereford progressed into the 20th Century, the partnership of Medical Officer and Public Health Inspector oversaw the health, safety and welfare of the citizens of Hereford, whilst at the same time using changing public health legislation to improve their living and working conditions. In 1935, the staff of the City Health Department undertook nearly four thousand inspections and served over five hundred notices. By this time only forty eight houses in Hereford were supplied by well water and one hundred and eleven not served by the main sewerage system. Action taken included demolition of unfit houses, repair and improvement of rented houses, abatement of nuisances, monitoring of offensive trades, inspection of food manufacturing and retail premises, sampling of drinking waters, foods, swimming baths water and milk, meat inspection, condemnation of unfit foods, and examination of foodstuffs intended for human consumption.

It is interesting to note that at that time Hereford boasted 29 warehouses to serve a population of 24,163, testimony to the changes in food production and retailing that have taken place over the intervening years. Over the next two years major Acts of Parliament on Public Health, Housing and Food consolidated and extended the powers available to Local Authorities. These extended powers were diligently and systematically employed over the next 30 years, during which Hereford's population expanded to nearly 45,000 and diseases such as typhoid, diphtheria, tuberculosis and whooping cough virtually disappeared.

During the 1960's and 1970's the aspirations and expectations of the population were reflected in improvements in housing standards with many grant-aided schemes providing previously sub-standard homes with modern amenities and comprehensive repairs. ▷

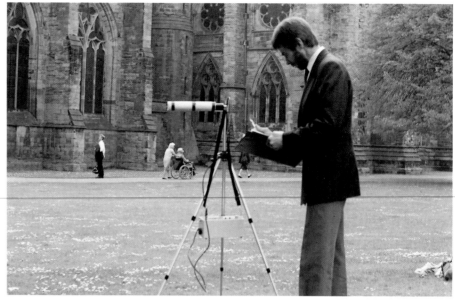

Measuring background gamma radiation.

Public Health in Hereford Today

A century of progress has seen many changes in Hereford City. Today's sophisticated and bustling City would seem strange indeed to a resident of the 1880's with safe piped water supplies, mains drainage properly treated, many types of fresh and preserved foods not then even dreamed of, industrial processes on a large scale and a great sophistication requiring equally sophisticated pollution control systems and, perhaps most striking would be the noise generated by today's lifestyle.

Hereford City Council's Health and Leisure Department encompasses a number of functions, including those carried out by its Environmental Health Division. The role of this division can be summarised as responsibility for:-
General Public Health, including abatement of nuisances, infectious disease investigations and enforcement, food safety including food hygine and meat inspection, health and safety at work, pollution and noise control, private sector housing standards, public conveniences, pest control, animal welfare, caravan site standards and health education. In addition to its role safeguard-

ing the public in these areas, the department also advises other council Departments and a variety of statutory and non-statutory bodies on environmental implications of such matters as planning applications, proposed schemes and policies. The Inspector of Nuisances of a century ago would find strange indeed the sophisticated equipment and convoluted legislation (tempered by a century of case law) employed by today's Environ-

mental Health Officers. The public's expectations constantly rise, and with ever new and diverse threats to our health and the environment, there are always new challenges to be met. The Black Death crawled slowly across Europe in the Middle Ages, AIDS travels first class by supersonic jet. A holidaymaker can contract typhoid in North Africa and be back at his job making pork pies in Hereford two days later! □

A

MADE IN HEREFORD

THE CITY'S SAXON AND NORMAN COINAGE

From the reign of Aethelstan (924 - 939) to the early Middle Ages, silver coins were minted in Hereford on behalf of the King. The moneyers were craftsmen specially appointed for the task and it is interesting to note that their names were usually Anglo Saxon in origin. This continued after the Norman conquest as Saxon craftsmanship was well respected.

There were 76 towns, at this time, minting coinage for the Monarch. The coin in use was the penny, the denarius, in Latin, named after the small Roman coin of the same name. Approximately half an inch in diameter, the penny was made of almost pure silver. However, the silver content was debased during the reign of Henry I and the Civil War of Stephen.

The obverse portrayed the Monarch with a crowned head and crudely depicted face. Around the head are grouped many letters which are difficult to decipher at first. On coins of William I the inscription would read *PILLEMUS REX*, as the Saxon and Normans used the letter "P" as we use the letter "W". On the reverse, there is always a cross which, in effect, divided the coin into four segments, and around the edge there is the moneyer's name and place of manufacture, e.g. AESTAN ON HERE (Aestan in Hereford).

The coins are divided into various types stylistically, by numismatists, and are dated accordingly, e.g. there are eight basic types for William I, five types for William II, fifteen types for Henry I and only four types for Stephen. These types vary considerably, such as the *"Bonnet"* type (1086 - 1071), so called because the Crown is shaped like a bonnet; or the *"Paxs"* type (1086 - 1087), so called because of the letters in the segments of the cross on the reverse. Some types are named after the form of the Cross on the reverse such as the *Profile/cross Fleury* (1066 - 1068) or the *cross Pattée and Fleury* (1096 - 1099). Other types are named after the hoard in which they are found, such as the Watford type or rare Awbridge type, dating from the reign of Stephen.

How the coins were made

All Anglo Saxon, Norman and medieval coins were made by the hammered process. The rough silver coin blank was held between two dies by a long pair of tongs and a heavy blow was given with a mallet. The bottom die had the obverse design of the coin engraved upon it, whilst the top die was placed over the reverse of the coin. The last hammered coins to be struck in England were the small penny, twopenny, threepenny and fourpenny pieces of 1662. At this time milling was introduced in order to halt coin clipping. Over the years, unscrupulous moneyers would clip pieces of silver from the coin edges and store the silver for their own benefit. This was an offence punishable by death or, at least mutilation. The right hand was cut off and nailed to the wall of the workshop as a warning to others! However, the silver penny could be cut in half to make a halfpenny, or in quarters to make a feorthling or farthing. Only the Crown could order coins to be minted and counterfeiting is still a serious crime.

Where was Hereford's Mint or Mints?

The simple answer is we do not know - it has not been discovered through archaeological excavations, so far. The earliest Saxon Mint may have been near the Cathedral and the Norman Mint would probably have been with the confines of the King's Castle on Castle Green. The name of the Mint was not spelled out in full; Hereford was shortened to *HERE, HEREFOR, HEREF* or just *HER*. During the reign of William the Conqueror and William Rufus, the moneyers were Aegelric, Aeglwine, Aelfwi, Aestan, Brihtric, Edwine, Godric, Hethewi, Lifstan, Ordwi, Wulfwine, and in the reign of Henry I five recorded moneyers are Adebrant, Edric, Edwine, Ravenswert and Saric. Perhaps one day we will find the City Mint with the remains of silver blanks, dies and fragments of crucible. But until then, the skill of these early craftsmen moneyers can be admired in the City Museum's Collection, their fine Saxon names recorded for posterity.

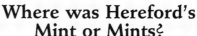

B

C

D

HEREFORD THEATRES
AND TEMPLES OF THE MOVING IMAGE

Hereford's theatrical tradition is presumed to have commenced in the early Middle Ages when Interludes and Plays took place in the City's churches. Bishop Trilleck (1344 - 61) later prohibited all such plays throughout the diocese because by then "the hearts of the faithful are drawn aside to vanities". These plays were probably similar to the Corpus Christi pageants which were staged in the streets on waggons, organised by the Guilds. The pageants began with Adam and Eve and ended after the Crucifixion with St. Catherine and her three Tormentors! The Guilds' full programme is known from the City's archives for 1503.

The earliest theatre building was erected on the West side of Broad Street in the second half of the 18th century, probably on the same site as the later *Kemble Theatre*. It was described in the 1827 City Guide as *"handsome, with prediments adorned with busts of Shakespeare, Powell and Garrick"*. The Manager was obliged to obtain permission from the Mayor and Aldermen for sixty nights of performances within a year. At the age of seventeen, Sarah Siddons played in *"Beaux Stratagem"* together with both her parents. Other notable performers of the day included Mrs. Clive, Mr. Powell, Mr. Macready and the Miss Barton Company, who trod the boards of this fine theatre which was demolished in 1857 and a Corn Exchange built in its place. The Corn Exchange was used as a makeshift theatre for about fifty years and Mrs. Howard Paul is reported to have brought the house down by her rendering of *"The Marseillaise"*, suitably draped in a tricolour, at the time of the Franco-Prussion War. A Company of freed slaves came to perform *"Uncle Tom's Cabin"* and was well received in the City. The building was extended and renamed *"The Kemble"* in 1911, although the front portion continued to be used as a corn exchange on Wednesday market day. With a panelled pillared interior, decorated in gold and pink, it opened with the *"Pantomine Rehersal"* given by The Amateur Theatricals in aid of the Herefordshire General Hospital, which benefited to the extent of £100. In 1951 it became a combined cinema and theatre until its closure in 1961 and, sadly, demolition followed in 1963. *"The Kemble"* is a place of magical memories for very many Herefordians.

The "Garrick" Theatre, in Widemarsh Street, had a chequered history. Built in 1882 as a Forresters Hall, it was called the *"Theatre Royal"* in 1900, but nine years later became *"The Garrick"* under the management of a Mr. Henderson. Famous Shakespearean actors visited the city, including Osmond Tearle, Herman Vezin and, of course the Bandmann-Palmer Co., where Mrs. Patrick Campbell received her early training. Edmund Compton, father of Fay Compton, also played comedy here.

Burlesques, reviews and Adelphi Melodramas all came to the Garrick, much loved by Herefordians. Tragedy struck, however, in 1916, when fire broke out and eight little girls died whilst taking part in a Charity Concert for the Troops. The theatre was destroyed but rebuilt soon after.

During the second World War, the building became the A.R.P. Headquarters and continued as a much patronised cinema. In 1946, it became the County Library, closing in 1974. Four years later, the auditorium was demolished, disclosing original decor of pink and gold with guilded mouldings, but the richly detailed serpentine front and the ornately capitalled cast iron columns from the balcony were salvaged for later incorporation in the *Nell Gwynne Theatre*. The City Council's multi-storey car park now stands on the site and continues to bear Garrick's name; perhaps theatrical ghosts move amongst the twentieth century metal occupants of their former 'home'!

The *Palladium*, in Berrington Street, still remembered by many Herefordians, was originally built as a private chapel in 1787, and a hundred years later became the Beethovan Hall, a fine Parlour Piano and organ showroom for Messrs. Heins. Just prior to the first World War, it became the *Palladium Theatre* and as early as 1919, films were also shown. In 1946, it was renamed the *County Theatre* with theatrical performances on weekdays and films on Sundays. In the 1950's it was used for dances, bingo and roller skating and for a short period a small ice rink was installed. In the 1960's it became the *Regal Cinema*, and today a bingo hall, the building having been much restored.

The *Alhambra*, a forgotten city theatre, stood in Bridge Street, the position occupied by the Crystal Rooms today. Built in the 1830's as part of the premises of the Royal Oak Inn, the theatre was approached from Gwynne Street, only a few yards from the reputed birthplace of Nell Gwynne. Fully galleried on three sides, this small theatre was used mainly as a music hall, but also for plays and even *"spelling bees"*! By 1890, it had become a corn warehouse for Messrs. Franklin Barnes and was demolished in 1936.

In 1909, *St. George's Hall* was built at the end of Bewell Street, initially as a roller skating rink, but also served as a Playhouse and used by visiting companies. However, it was condemned as structurally defective before the elaborate frontage design could be built. It then became a garage; and the site now lies under the Ring Road.

Herefordians also had a chance to view large visiting productions at the *Drill Hall*, Friar Street, built in the 1890's. Musical comedies such as *"Floradora"* and *"The Shop Girl"* and even *"The Carl Rosa Opera Company Productions"* were firm favourites. However, in the early days there was no heating, so the audience viewed performances clustered around an open stove. Presumably, the players had their 'art' to keep them warm!

Hereford was without a theatre for many years after the demise of *"The Kemble"*. Plans were devised in the early 1970's for a theatre in St. Owen Street but did not come to fruition.

However, in 1975, a group of enthusiasts launched a "self-help" conversion scheme to utilise the redundant Swimming Baths in Edgar Street. Built in 1929, the old baths re-opened on 5th March, 1979 as "The Nell Gwynne Theatre and Arts Centre". The building works were undertaken by local theatre enthusiasts, following the setting up of a Charitable Trust and the launch of a £100,000 Building Fund. Staffed mainly by volunteers, the theatre was used by all the local amateur groups and also professional visiting companies and from time to time, films were also shown. The "Nell Gwynne" closed in 1984 and re-opened on 1st April, 1985 as "The New Hereford Theatre" managed by the Stennett Organisation with financial assistance from the City Council. Used by local groups, visiting companies, and also as a cinema, this year sees developments at the "New" to include a Studio Theatre which will accomodate 'workshop' and smaller productions especially with a view to the encouragement of youth theatre.

Hereford is fortunate to also have a fine *Studio Theatre* at the Cathedral School, and studio theatre space under construction at the Herefordshire College of Art.

INTERIOR OF THE KEMBLE C. 1911

'THE CHERRY ORCHARD' - THE WYE PLAYERS 1968 PRODUCTION AT THE GREENSLADE HALL, YMCA. STAGE AND COSTUME DESIGN BY MALCOLM STEED, NOW AT COVENT GARDEN.

Hereford's Amateur Tradition

Over the last 100 years, very many Herefordians have trodden the boards. The Operatic Companies have already been mentioned, but a wealth of Amateur Companies have flourished over the years, like the Phoenix, the Cory Christy Nigger Minstrels, the Bon-Optimists Concert Party and the Pantomine Societies. Especially remembered is the Wiggin Recreation Club Pantomine Group (now evolved into the Hereford Amateur Pantomine Society) who performed at Wiggin's own Theatre for many years.

Other groups, the Hereford County Players, the Holy Trinity Players and The Wye Players were and are widely supported. The latter, formerly the Y.M.C.A. Players, have achieved notable successes in the British Drama League over the years, and even represented Britain in Drama Festivals in Holland and France. Currently, they present four productions a year in the City.

Amateur performing groups grow from strength to strength. No less than fourteen, including the Hereford Players, were entered for this year's 52nd County Drama Festival at the New Hereford Theatre. This is one of the longest running Drama Festivals in the Country, with a Golden Jubilee celebrated in March, 1987, and it is a preliminary round of the All England Theatre Festival.

Theatre in Hereford is indeed alive and well, with an enthusiastic, talented young generation, well able to carry the Thespian tradition into the twenty first century.   ▷

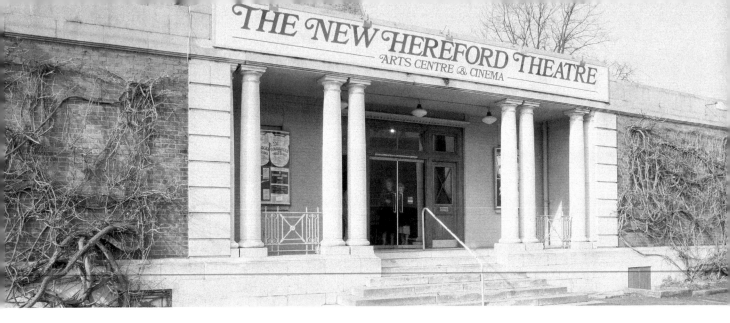

Temples of the Moving Image - Hereford Cinemas

As we have seen, most of Hereford's theatres were also used as cinemas over the years together with halls, like the Drill Hall and the Co-Operative Hall in St. Owen Street. But Hereford also had two custom-built *"temples of the moving image"* reflecting the height of 1930's style and elegance.

The *Odeon,* in High Town, now lost to the Maylord Orchards develop-ment, was opened on 17th April, 1937, by the Mayor Councillor Mrs. Luard. Designed by Roland Sutwell, the Odean became a focal point for young and old. The Band of the Scots Guards played at its grand opening, and Will Hay starred in *"Good Morning, Boys".* Oscar Deutch did indeed *Entertain Our Nation"!*

The *Ritz* Cinema, now *"The Classic",* in Commercial Road, is today a shadow of its former size, albeit comfortable and compact. It was designed by Leslie H. Kemps and was opened on 10th January, 1938, by the Mayor, Councillor F.W. Allcock. There were 290 stadium seats at 1/- and 722 seats in the stalls at 6d. Jeanette MacDonald and Nelson Eddy starred in *"Maytime"* and the famous Wilfred Southworth at the Mighty Compton Organ was the hit of the opening evening! □

Music Making
in Hereford

Hereford Amateur Operatic Society
Scene from "My Fair Lady"

Hereford is noteworthy for being the birthplace of actors and actresses rather than musicians, however we have John Bull the Tudor organist of Hereford Cathedral, subsequently of the Chapel Royal and Professor of Music in London before moving on - he presumably did not suit Scottish King James - to Brussels and, finally, Antwerp: a bird of passage like many whose musical career has brought them to the Cathedral, but a man whose keyboard playing gives him a place of great importance in the history of its development.

By the reign of Queen Victoria, higher standards of living brought opportunity for cultural pursuits among a much wider section of the population, so that musical societies were taking a more corporate and self-conscious form. Not surprisingly, it was the Cathedral, with its long-established tradition of "Music Meeting", which gave rise to the formation of the Hereford Choral Society in the year of the Queen's accession. Only a few years before, the organist and composer Samuel Sebastian Wesley had been constrained to compose an anthem for a choir which comprised a few choirboys and the Dean's butler: it is still very much in the repertoire. Not surprisingly, therefore, the newly-formed Choral Society under John Hunt appeared frequently as an adjunct to the Cathedral choir on occasions such as the foundation-laying ceremony for the new St. Martin's Church. John Hunt's successors included George Robertson Sinclair - one of Edward Elgar's portrayals in 'Enigma Variations' under whom the Society's ranks swelled to unprecedented heights, never yet surpassed. Sir Percy Hull, whose reign as conductor extended between the two world wars and beyond recalls, as a young assistant, helping Sinclair to decide whether a Festival Te Deum and Benedictus Elgar had brought along, would be acceptable for the 1897 Three Choirs. "Hull and I will decide after dinner. . . . ." Sir Percy was followed in turn by Meredith Davies - who later conducted the first performance of the War Requiem for Benjamin Britten - Melville Cook and Richard Lloyd. The present incumbent, Roy Massey, presides over a flourishing society whose 150th anniversary concert featured Beethoven's Missa Solemnis accompanied by the Royal Liverpool Philharmonic Orchestra. Roy Massey's international reputation as an organ recitalist, has given considerable impetus to the regular series of summer recitals using the magnificent, and recently restored "Father Willis" Cathedral organ.

The latter half of the present Century has witnessed great expansion in the number of amateur groups dedicated to choral and vocal music. These include the Hereford Madrigal Society - the Hereford Chamber Choir, the Britten Singers, the Hereford Church Singers, Renaissance (who perform in period costume) and the Christian Chorale who, under the auspices of Hereford Christian Council, perform Handelian and other oratorio and play a chorus role in religious drama. Other groups have also been in evidence, such as the Monday Singers and the Hereford Carollers. The male-choir scene has been well represented by the Hereford Male-voice Choir, the Railway Choir and the Hereford Police Choir which latter body, founded 32 years ago by Freeman Newton, Chief Constable of Hereford and himself a keen amateur singer, continues to thrive with 80 or more members under its conductor, Alan Taylor.

Amateur operatic productions have flowered continuously since the turn of the Century. The Hereford Operatic Society was founded in 1898, its first President being Sir John Cotterell Bt, who was succeeded by Sir John Arkwright, and it is the sixth oldest operatic society in the country still in existence. During its lifetime it has encompassed productions of virtually the whole of the repertoire accessible to an amateur group. In 1915 British Red Cross and the Order of St. John were beneficiaries of a special event in aid of the War effort, whose programme spanned a matinee and an evening, concluding with 'Trial by Jury'. Alfred Brook was the Society's conductor for several decades.

The Hereford Gilbert and Sullivan Operatic Society evolved, after the Second War, from earlier productions at the Holy Trinity Institute under the auspices of the Vicar - later Prebendary Snell, Mayor of Hereford - where 'Merrie England" was staged in 1937. The productions of the post-war years remain in the mind, featuring some outstandingly talented Gilbertian characterisations by Ken Williams, ably supported by Sidney Roberts, Jim Perkins, Ella Fardon, Neville Wiggins, Doris Webster - who later founded the Hereford Savoy Singers - Mary Long and a host of others, including Percy Arrowsmith who was also for many years Secretary of the Choral Society.

A tradition of orchestral playing in what might have been regarded as a provincial backwater owes something in origin to the Three Choirs Festival, and it is not until the 1920's that this triennial event in Hereford came to rely on fully professional orchestras as such. The Herefordshire

INCO ALLOYS INTERNATIONAL

The Hereford factory of Inco Alloys Ltd. was first established in the 1950s.

Today, employing over 1,200 local people, it is the Company's European headquarters, serving customers in Britain, Western Europe, the Middle East, Australia, Asia and Africa.

In 1988 the Company announced a new £12 million investment in equipment, part of a total of over £30 million invested in Hereford over the past five years.

The nickel-based alloys made at the Wiggin Works, the high-powered production equipment, the research laboratories, and the skills of the people who work for the Company keep Inco Alloys International at the forefront of European metals technology.

INCO ALLOYS INTERNATIONAL

> Philharmonic Society was actually formed in 1836, one year before the Choral Society. Orchestral playing was nurtured and encouraged none more so than by the Heins family whose music business in Broad Street, spanning almost a century, many people will remember - a veritable institution of its time. Nurturing on a more domestic scale included a house at the foot of Aylestone Hill where for many years in the not-too-distant past Frederika Richardson hosted, in a possibly more spacious and possibly less affluent age, amateur quartet playing whose participants included Norah Parker, sister of the poet-laureate and a pupil of Elgar, and my own mother who played the 'cello', and this practice has been continued in recent time by Lady Hull, Peter and Marjorie Baker and others: when one thinks of the people concerned, it seems to have encouraged longevity! During a lean period after the Second War - when it was difficult to find a violin teacher in the county - the Herefordshire Community Council, led by Muriel Fildes, fostered music and other activities among the rural communities in an 'arts-for-all' initiative which, led among other things, to the formation of the Practice Orchestra for the less adept but improving, which has continued as a benefit to the community for the past 40 years. Amateur activity is also channeled into the City of Hereford Band and Youth Band, while the St. John's Recorder Group caters for these particular instruments.

In 1888 the Herefordshire Philharmonic Society was superseded by the Herefordshire Orchestral Society which has continued to give pleasure to many, with only intermittent periods of inactivity largely attributable to war and its aftermath. In its earlier days it was customary for two performances of its concerts to be given: one, in the afternoon, for the country people, and one on the evening of the following day for the townsfolk. The National Anthem was played at the commencement of the first and on conclusion of the second. An apochryphal story relates of a tuba player, Paul Rochard, who drew a deep anticipatory breath at the start of the evening concert - and caught Dr. Sinclair's eye just in time!

The Hereford String Orchestra, since its formation 30 years ago by Ronald Collett, Headmaster of Fairfield School, Peterchurch, has grown in stature and accomplishment with the passage of time. Numbering some 30 members, it has been directed variously by two Assistant Organists before they moved on to senior posts: Roger Fisher to Chester and, most recently, David Briggs to Truro. In the intervening years the work of building up the Orchestra's repertoire and levels of attainment fell to Julie Hollingworth for whom the performances of Finizi's Clarinet Concerto and 'Dies Natalis' constituted landmarks in the Orchestra's development.

The only organisation which exists to promote professional concerts and recitals on a regular basis is the Hereford Concert Society. 'Celebrity' concerts began to be held soon after the War, largely on the initiative of Peter Whitehead, Director of Education and Editha Jennings, Principal of the (then) Training College. Memorable among these was a Recital by Kathleen Ferrier just at the commencement of her short meteoric, career. The organisation was initially known as the Hereford Concert Club. Latterly, the Society's programmes have included concerts by the now well established English String Orchestra. Whilst its activities are mainly centred around the Great Hall of the Bishop's Palace, an elegant and much-needed recent addition to the limited choice of available venues, whose value can hardly be over-estimated, for larger audiences the Assembly Rooms of both the Town Hall and the Shirehall are the obvious choices, the largest of these having now become too small for the size of audience needed to support a full-blown choral concert with professional orchestra. Hereford has been fortunate to enjoy frequent visits by Midlands-based Orchestra da Camera which, under its Leader, Kenneth Page, regularly fills the accompanying role for the many and varied, works performed by the Choral Society as well as giving concerts in its own right. In recent years there have been two 'Hereford Wakes', summer festivals, providing a variety of entertainment, including music, for the local community, and in 1980 Hereford was host to an Elgar Festival arranged by Philomusica of Gloucestershire. Over the years the Cathedral School has figured prominently among schools in Hereford which have provided enhanced opportunity for young people to present a range of musical activity to the public, and a Hereford Youth Orchestra is directed by the County Music Inspector. At the same time a series of professional concerts in aid of the Hereford Waldorf School added richly to the fare already available. The coming of the Royal National College for the Blind to Hereford has, under its accomplished Musical Director, added a further interesting dimension of activity for those in search of culture. Impetus towards musical attainment for all ages has for many years been provided by the annual Herefordshire Competitive Festival, held until recently under the auspices of the Community Council, having started life in 1930, on the initiative of the then Director of Education as the 'Musical Competitive Festival' over which judges of the eminence of such as the late Herbert Howells have presided.

Hereford also enjoys a fair choice of popular music and there does not seem to be any shortage of talent. In particular, the fairly recent enhancement of public house amenity by groups consisting of several players is well advanced in this city. 'Blake's Three' is a prime example of such entertainment and the group enjoys wide support with its repertoire ranging from baroque to rock. A middle-of-the-road approach is evident in the performances of 'Scoop', while 'Black Velvet' is more representative of the Beatles era. Country and Western groups, such as the Roger Wood Duo, enjoy wide support also, while the Booth Hall lends its name to a music club. In addition to much vibrant local activity, 'Whole Music' is now in business to bring the world's music to Hereford - from nine different countries including Third World so far. The organisation seeks to promote concerts, dances and workshops, with particular emphasis on schools.

POETS & PAINTERS, SAINTS & SINNERS

The names of famous Herefordians and 'Honorary' Herefordians who lived and worked in the City are well in woven in the tapestry of History.

Some lived here for a short time, like **David Garrick** (1712 - 1779), who was born at the 'Angel', Widemarsh Street, was baptised at All Saints Church, and soon moved on, in his case to Lichfield, and future fame and fortune.

Pretty, witty, **Nell Gwynne** (1650 - 1687), the actress and Mistress of Charles II, is also claimed as Hereford's own. Reputed to have been born in Pipewell Lane, now Gwynne Street, she left Hereford a young girl, never to return, as far as we know. But her Grandson, **James Beauclerk** came to Hereford as Bishop, for forty years and is buried here.

Roger Kemble was born in Hereford in 1721, founding the Kemble acting dynasty. Most of his children, including the most famous, Sarah Siddons, acted here, as did Roger himself and his wife, Sarah. Although they led a perapatetic existence, as strolling players, Hereford was their base, and a plaque in Church Street records this at the entrance to Leicester Place.

Many painters visited the city to paint the Cathedral and the River Wye, men such as **J.M.W. Turner, Thomas Girtin, Edward Dayes** and the **Varleys, John** and **Cornelius**, their work well represented in the City's collections. Others like **David Cox** (in Hereford 1814 - 27) and his pupil, **Joseph Murray Ince** (1806 - 1859), lived and worked in the city, together with their great friend, **Edward Smith** (1795 - 1879).

Native artists, like **Brian Hatton** (1887 - 1916) are well represented in the City Art Galleries, as is the work of **John Ward** (1917 -), Hereford's Royal Academician. One of the most interesting artists who recorded the City in the late 18th and early 19th century was **James Wathen**, "Jemmy the Sketcher", a former glover, who travelled to India, China and even St. Helena, yet died at Aylestone House on Aylestone Hill.

"NELL GWYNNE'S FIRST INTRODUCTION TO KING CHARLES II."

A well - known family of artists, **Edmund Gill** and his three sons, **William, Edmund** and **George**, all lived in the city in Berrington Street and St. Owen Street, in the first half of the 19th century. George was also born in the city, before the family moved to Ludlow.

St. Thomas Cantilupe, (1218 - 82) Bishop and former Chancellor of England and Chancellor of Oxford, leads the famous Clerics associated with the City. Thirteenth century Nicholas of Hereford, and Miles Smith in the early 16th century, both worked on translating the Bible. Others, like Catholic **Humphrey Ely** and **Richard Gardiner** in the late 16th century, were renowned for their sermons.

We also find poet **Walter Map** or **Mapes** in the 12th century, a contemporary of **Giraldus Cambrensis** (who visited Hereford in 1188). **Roger of Hereford** completes this group of native erudite men, with his works on astronomical tables such as the **Theoretica Planetarium**.

St. Ethelbert, Hereford's royal Saint, was buried in the Cathedral some time after his murder in 792. His tomb was renowned for miracles, particularly in the 12th and 13th centuries. Giraldus Cambrensis, in his 'Life of St. Ethelbert', helped shape the legend. ▷

▷ Hereford's Saint was **St. John Kemble**, priest and martyr, who was executed on Windemarsh Common on 22nd August, 1679 at the age of eighty. His last request for a pipe tobacco was granted which he shared with the executioner.

Hereford also produced well - known poets such as **Thomas Traherne** (1637 - 74), later a vicar of Credenhill, and **John Davies** (1565 - 81) the Critic. Traherne's work was lost for many years, but is now compared to that of Donne and Herbert.

Alfred Watkins (1855 - 1935), photographer, antiquarian and inventor, is well - known outside the city, not only for his inventions, such as the Bee Meter, but also for his work on ley lines - "The Old Straight Track". Other well - known photographers include the **Bustin** family of Palace Yard and **F.C. Morgan,** former librarian and curator and later Chief Steward of the City of Hereford. We are lucky to have their wonderful collections of glass plate negatives and prints depicting the city and its surroundings in the Library, County Record Office and City Museum collections.

A group of unusual Herefordians include the well - known broadcaster **Gilbert Harding,** who was born in the city whilst his Mother was Matron of the Workhouse.

The 'Father of the Indian Army', **General Stringer Lawrence** (1697 - 1775), of the East India Company, was born in the city and baptised in All Saints, but lived most of his life abroad. His memorial can be seen in Westminster Abbey.

Fownhope's **Tom Spring**, born Thomas Winter, the Boxing Champion of All England 1823 - 24, lived in the city as Landlord of the historic Booth Hall, no doubt fully able to deal with a riotus public house.

Children's author, **Elinor Brent-Dyer** (1894 - 1969), of the 'Chalet School' fame, had her own school, the Margaret Roper School in the city at Lichfield House. Her books are still read all over the World and are much collected.

Finally, a famous four-legged Herefordian, **Dan**, the bulldog, owned by Dr. George Roberts Sinclair, the celebrated Cathedral Organist. Dan is portrayed in No. 11 of Elgar's 'Enigma' Variations, and is buried in the garden of his home, 20 Church Street, Hereford.

We may not have been established for 800 years, but **The Hereford Times** has been serving the local community since 1832

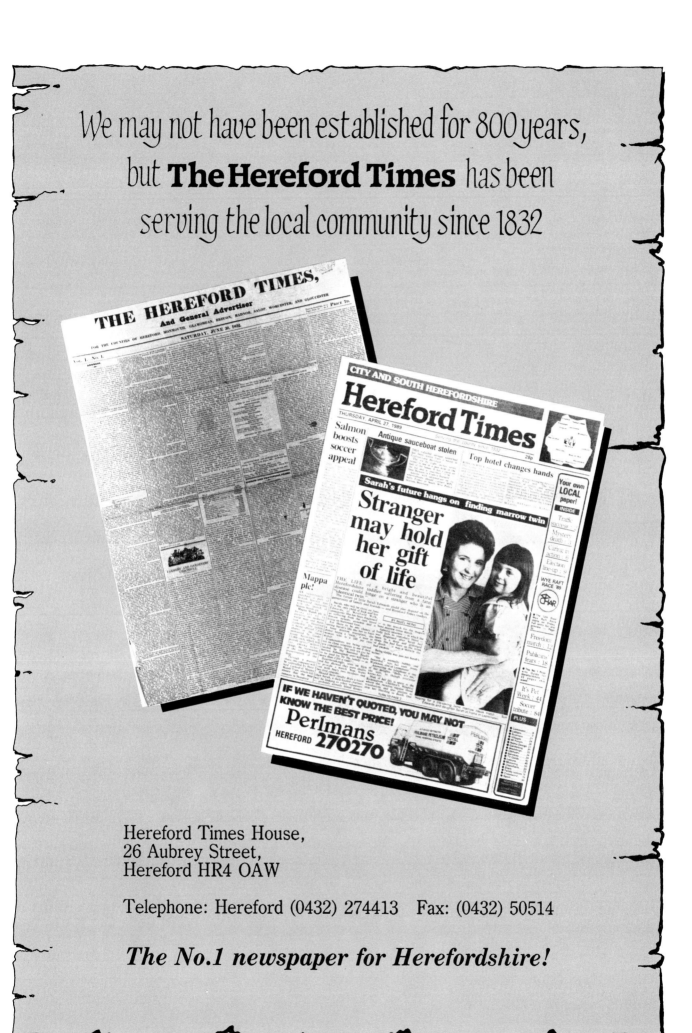

Hereford Times House,
26 Aubrey Street,
Hereford HR4 OAW

Telephone: Hereford (0432) 274413   Fax: (0432) 50514

The No.1 newspaper for Herefordshire!

Edward Elgar's Hereford

One October day in the year 1905, an observer in St Owens' Street would have seen a small party, headed by the Mayor and his Town Clark, emerge from the Town Hall and drive away from town, towards Eign Hill. It was destined for a fine stuccoed Victorian mansion on the summit aptly named Plâs Gwyn. And their mission was one of the oddest in the Corporation's history - to invite its new resident although not a Councillor, to become the next Mayor of Hereford, as the "highest office in their power".

He would certainly have been the city's most famous Mayor, for he was the country's greatest composer since Purcell - Sir Edward Elgar, newly knighted, already world-famous for his Enigma Variations, The Dream of Gerontius, and the tune to Land of Hope and Glory. And he and Lady Elgar had chosen Hereford as their home.

Elgar's connections with Hereford went back much earlier than this, however. His mother was born in the county - at Pontshill, near Ross - and as young violinist he accompanied his father in various local orchestras, including that for the "Three Choirs".

As such he soon encountered a young Irishman named George Robertson Sinclair, who was appointed Cathedral organist - and therefore ex officio Three Choirs conductor - in 1890. Elgar travelled regularly from nearby Malvern to perform, and a close artistic and personal friendship grew up between the two musicians. Sinclair introduced new Elgar works to the festivals, and many others would be tried out at the organist's house near the Cathedral in Church Street.

The weekend after beginning his Variations on an Original Theme - a series of musical portraits of his friends - in October 1898, Elgar stayed at Sinclair's, and they took Dan, the organist's bull-terrier, for a walk along the Wye. Dan managed to tumble in, and Sinclair challenged the composer to set the incident to music. Elgar combined Dan's paddling and Sinclair's organ-pedalling with the "Enigma" theme: the result became part of the work which would rocket him to fame.

Sinclair's surviving Visitor's Book for the house contains a whole set of other whimsical sketches of the dog, written during the composer's frequent stays, which Elgar ▷

DR. SINCLAIR AND SIR EDWARD ELGAR SEATED IN THE GARDEN OF 20, CHURCH STREET WITH DAN THE DOG.

dubbed The Moods of Dan (Illustrated). They subtitles like "Dan triumphant (after a fight)" and "Dan wistful".

Some of these also later found their way, brilliantly orchestrated into somewhat more exalted places, like the overture In the South and even The Dream of Gerontius. They provide a further glimpse of Elgar's often tortuous creative processes.

Dan died in 1903, and his owner erected a memorial headstone above his grave in the garden, which still exists.

During the Elgars' residence at Plâs Gwyn, from 1904 - 1911, Elgar produced most of the other works by which he is remembered - the Introduction and Allegro, the Kingdom, the Pomp and Circumstance March No. 4 (dedicated to Sinclair); the Violin Concerto and the two Symphonies which secured his reputation as a major composer. The house became a place of pilgrimage for fellow-musicians. He had a composing-study on the ground floor, but inspiration would often come during walks by the Wye, or cycle-rides in the lanes and fields. He also dabbled in chemistry, and one famous occasion - depicted in Ken Russell's famous BBC film Elgar - nearly blew the house up!

Following the enormous popularity of the "great works" Lady Elgar had forecast would be written here, the Elgars were finally forced to move to the capital. Asked if he were now in clover in his new Hampstead house, he replied ruefully, "I might as well be in Hereford".

He continued, nevertheless, to attend every year the Three Choirs Festival, and notably several major works would be performed under his baton to enraptured audiences. In 1927 he composed for the opening procession the Civic Fanfare. His last public appearance, sadly, was at the 1933 Hereford meeting; four months later he died in Worcester.

Elgar - or rather his friends - ultimately decided he would have to put composing before conducting the City Council's business for a year! But he remains Hereford's most illustrious, and probably best-loved, former citizen.

45

The three choirs festival

No one really seems to know when the three choirs of Hereford, Gloucester and Worcester Cathedrals first all met 'to make musick together' but the earliest authenticated date is 1718 and since a local newspaper advertisement in 1719 addressed 'Members of the yearly Musical Assembly of these Parts' it is generally assumed thast the event was already of some years' standing by then. The annual 'Music Meeting' held in ▷

◁ rotation in the tree cathedral cities, and from 1838 called 'The Three Choirs Festival', is now quite the oldest annual musical festival being held ▽

anywhere in the World. To begin with, the occasion comprised two days of sacred works only, performed within the choir. Oratorios and other 'secular' works were always arranged elsewhere until the unprecendented step was taken in 1759 at Hereford of allowing Handel's new oratorio 'Messiah' to be performed actually in the Cathedral. This created a precedent for many other cathedrals and locally the scope of the Music Meeting expanded quickly to the point when, in 1834 when S.S. Wesley was Organist and Festival Conductor at Hereford, the performances moved out into the nave. Gloucester followed suit in 1835 and thereafter the number of performers steadily increased. Not everyone was happy about the development of the Festival however and the whole affair came almost to an end in 1875 at Worcester due to misgivings and resistance by the Dean and Chapter. Emotions ran high, effigies were burned there (not so far considered at Hereford!) but happily continuity was restored the following year, due in part to initiatives by the Mayor of Hereford.

Throughout the history of the Festival, Hereford has seen its share of special occasions and famous people, not least of whom was Edward Elgar. He regarded the Festival as 'the focal point of his year' for many years up to his final appearance as a conductor at the Hereford Festival in 1933, shortly before he died. Many other great musicians have visited the city to make music with the Three choirs no least in fulfulment of the long established aims of the encouragement of composers and the promotion of new works.

The place of Hereford in the annals of the 'Three Choirs' and of English Music will remain secure whilst their works and the memories of their performances last, and whilst all those involved in and around the City continue with such devotion and zeal to produce an event which, as one festival goer put it, "is unrivalled for its magic, its sense of belonging and continuous friendship and the great charm of its continuity of tradition". □

LEFT FESTIVAL CHORUS IN 1906.

ABOVE
THREE CHOIRS FESTIVAL 1933, L - R, H.K. FOSTER, DR. PERRY HULL, SIR EDWARD ELGAR AND SIR IVOR ATKINS.

BARCLAYS BANK PLC

HEREFORD BRANCH

IS PLEASED TO BE

ASSOCIATED WITH THE

CITY OF HEREFORD'S

800th ANNIVERSARY

CELEBRATIONS

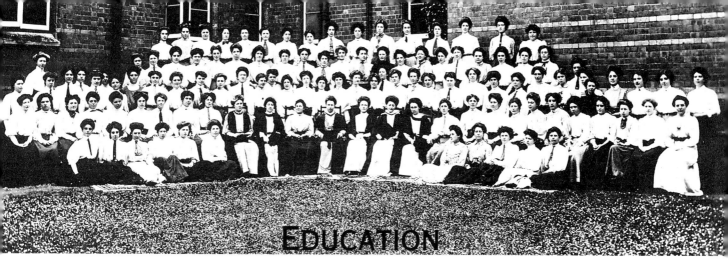

EDUCATION

The Church and the cathedral were probably providing education in Hereford from an early date but the most ancient foundation documented is that of the Cathedral School which was founded in 1381 by Bishop Gilbert. This was to give free education to the sons of poor citizens of Hereford but paying pupils were admitted in 1665 to augment the schoolmaster's salary of £30 a year. The early school was situated in Old Schole Strete, now Harley Close and later in "the spacious and superb" Music Room at the side of the cathedral's west end. In 1804 the school moved into Castle Street and on to its present site in 1836. since then it has been remodelled several times until it is today an independent, co-educational school retaining its historic role in the education of choristers from the cathedral.

The Bluecoat Schools (1710) were another attempt to provide schooling for the poor and they were built outside the City Wall beyond Bye gate in the street that still has this name. The original blue uniform was discontinued when the charity funds ran dry. The 1827 building remains but the reorganisation of some schools in 1972 created a church-aided school providing comprehensive secondary education and now known as The Bishop of Hereford's Bluecoat School and relocated at Tupsley.

The Scudamore Endowed Schools were started in 1851 after much argument following an Act of Parliament in 1839. Funds amounting to £5,250 had accumulated from a legacy of £400 left by Lord James Scudamore in 1680 for the employment of poor people. They were rebuilt in 1912 after being sold to the Local Education Authority. Today they are a mixed primary school for the City area.

Parish schools were founded in the nineteenth century by the Church: St. Peter's (1836), St. Nicholas (1844), St. Martins (1859). All Saints' (1870) and, in the suburbs, Holmer and St. Paul's. Before these there had been the National schools in Eign Gate and numerous small private schools. A Catholic school, St. Francis Xavier's was started in 1835. It moved to various locations ending up in Berrington Street in 1875. A new building opened in Venn's Lane, almost a hundred years later, St. Owen's (1905) was built as a result of the 1902 Education Act which made Local Authorities responsible for providing elementary, secondary and technical education. This was an important act for it provided grammar school education for boys and girls when the Boys' High School (1912) and the Girls' High School (1915) opposite, opened in Widemarsh Street. During the 1960's and '70s secondary education was re-organised and schools were made comprehensive. Both the High Schools became the basis of the new Aylestone school in the buildings of the former Girls' High School.

One of the most interesting buildings in Hereford is that of the Royal College for the Visually Handicapped. It was built by F.R. Kempson in 1880 as a private school called the County College but when it closed in 1904 it became the first Ladies Training College for Elementary teachers under the 1902 Act and it continued as a mixed College of Education until 1977 when it closed. The new establishment is the only college of further education for visually handicapped students who come from all parts of Britain and from overseas. They are often to be seen confidently making their way into the city and are now very much part of the community.

Technical education was provided in a limited way by the elementary schools and the Arts and Crafts College on Castle Green. A purpose built Technical College opened in Folly Lane in 1954 and a new College of Art joined it next door in 1969. When the Sixth Form College was completed on the other side in 1973 a whole modern campus, of which Hereford is justly proud, was created for the education of young people. Many adults take advantage of the excellent facilities offered here to continue a tradition of Adult Education which began in the St. Peter's Literary Institute and the Mechanics' Institute in Church Street. Oxford University started extension lectures in 1884 and the Workers' Educational Association had a branch here after World War One, and still flourishes. Since then the Open University has produced many local graduates who helped themselves by taking up this new challenge.

In the ninteenth century there were many private schools in Hereford but the excellent education offered to today's children means only a select few flourish. Hereford is a long way from Universities and higher education but as a small City its citizens know how to make the most of what is offered.

□

THE BOYS' HIGH SCHOOL.

ABOVE
THE LADIES TRAINING COLLEGE BEFORE THE FIRST WORLD WAR.

800 Years of Policing Hereford City

Law enforcement in Charter Year 1189, as applicable to the City of Hereford, was a mixture of Anglo-Saxon and Danish Tribal Laws and Customs, a system, both personal and local, under which all members of a community accepted an obligation for the good behaviour of each other. Norman influence followed replacing the unpaid Officer of the Tything with their post of Constable.

The Statute of Winchester in 1285 re-affirmed the principle of local responsibility for policing a district, but made a distinction between town and rural policing. Watch-by-night and Ward-by-day was introduced to the City and was a combination of Constables elected annually, with Watch-men under their direction and appointment. Penalties were incurred for refusal to carry out their duties. The parish, controlled by its Vestry, was an important unit of local administration and during Tudor times its policing was carried out by Parish or Petty constables. The Stuart period saw the expansion of Towns and the number of Watchmen increased. From the reign of Charles II they were known as 'Charlies'. Taking the word in its modern idiom, regretably, many of them probably were. The image of very old men, long past active life, snoozing away in their Watch Boxes still remains.

Local Acts obtained from Parliament at the end of the eighteenth century giving Hereford City power to levy rates for Watching and Lighting etc., were applied in order to improve Watch standards by paying wages.

The early ninteenth century saw a break-down of policing in the small corporate towns. Corruption was rife and there was no liason or co-operation between the various bodies with a City responsible for its policing. In the case of Hereford there were three separate Constabulary officers - Corporation officials, Petty Constables for the Wards, and the Night Watchman.

A reforming Whig Government passed the Municipal Corporation Act 1835 which required the one hundred and seventy-eight Corporate Boroughs in England and Wales to elect a Town Council by popular franchise. They were required to form a Watch Committee within three weeks, and appoint sufficient numbers of fit men to

A policeman's lot . . . . .
Hereford police, 1893

be sworn in to act as Constables for preserving the peace by day and night, and preventing robberies. They would be paid out of rates and provided with uniform.

Accordingly on the last day of January 1836 the ten Corporation Officers relinquished the constabulary part of their various duties, and the eight Night Watchmen handed in their capes and lanthorns and quitted the Sentry Boxes. Constables in the Wards were not even mentioned.

Hereford City Police Force was formed on 1st February 1836 and was to serve the City for the next one hundred and eleven years, throughout six reigns and two major world wars. The original establishment was fixed at 17 and by 1856, because of a further Police Act appointing Inspectors of Constabulary and government ▽

There were only five Chief Officers; the first two both came from the Metropolitan Force (G. Adams and J. Davies) and held the rank of Superintendent. The title Head or Chief Constable was given to Mr. Frank Richardson (1882 - 1919). He was followed by Mr. T. Rawson who took charge for only seven years, but left a highly efficient Force with as smartly a turned-out body of men that could be desired.

The fifth and final Chief - Mr. Freeman Newton (1927 - 1947) combined the post with that of the County from 1929 onwards. He brought the Force into the twentieth century with improved housing, proper recruit training, mobile patrols and an up-to-date C.I.D. as well as District Beat Boxes and 'phone pillars for easier access to assistance by both police and public. ▽

On 31st March 1947, Hereford City Police Force, in company with forty-four other non-County Boroughs, ceased to operate in accordance with the Police Act 1946, and amalgamated within the County in which they were situated. Intense pride was felt by Hereford folk in their own local force, and a natural feeling of anxiety in its loss. The merger, however, went ahead very smoothly and on the following day, 1st April 1947, the whole of Hereford City Police area, plus part of the rural district around it became part of the newly constituated Central Division of the Herefordshire County Constabulary operating from Gaol Street, with Superintendent F. Wheatley in charge. 95% of the former city force continued to serve with the Division, the only difference from the public's point of view being the disappearance of the resplendent City helmet and uniform, into the more sombre clothing of the County Force.

A larger Police unit was formed on 1st October 1967 when Herefordshire Constabulary merged with the Police Forces of Shropshire, Worcestershire and Worcester City to become West Mercia Constabulary.

Hereford citizens were now under the protection of 'E' Division of the new Force which took in a much larger area consisting not only of Hereford City but also sub-divisions in Leominster and Ross.

A Chief Superintendent (Mr. C.W. Wallin) was in charge of this Division with Headquarters at Hafod Road, and the main Hereford Police Station still functioned as before.

In 1976 a brand new building was erected as Divisional Headquarters with all modern facilities and equipment necessary to cope with a rapidly expanding population and an ever increasing crime load and its prevention.

This continues to be so in 1989 and 800 years on from Charter Year, Hereford people have come to accept that their policing can only be carried out by larger Forces for today's criminal knows no boundaries and the cry of the old Watchman guarding the city walls calling out the time and state of the weather has long vanished into Hereford history. □

grants towards Force costs paid on receiving a Certificate of Efficiency, it reached twenty-two men. This figure slowly increased over the year's to peak at forty-nine all ranks just before the outbreak of War in 1939.

His responsibilities were heavy during the six years of the 1939 - 1945 war, and were carried out by those regulars not on active service, plus a large body of paid auxiliaries and a very supportive Special Constabulary.

POLICE CONTROLLING THE CROWDS WATCHING PRINCESS HENRY OF BATTENBURG ON 13TH MAY, 1902. SHE WAS ATTENDING A CATHEDRAL SERVICE TO UNVEIL THE WOMENS' MEMORIAL WINDOW IN MEMORY OF HER MOTHER, QUEEN VICTORIA. SHORTLY AFTERWARDS SHE UNVEILED THE FOUNDATION STONE OF THE NEW TOWN HALL IN ST. OWEN'S STREET.

A CELEBRATION OF CIDER

Although its traditions go back to Roman times, the first documentary evidence of English Cidermaking occurs during the reign of King John in 1205. Cider was certainly known to Chaucer and has proved efficacious against many of mans ills ever since. One of its great assets would appear to have been the encouragement of longevity!

"In 1609 when 'Hereford Towne shew like the best peopled Cittie. . . . The streetes swarmed with people. . . . . " This was the famous occasion when twelve men danced a Morris Dance in High Town, their combined ages making over twelve hundred years, "For what some wanted of 100 years, others exceeded. . . . . .and all were reported to be constant cider drinkers." "For a good wager, it were easie to find in that countie 400 persons more, within three ouer or vnder an hunder yeares."

"The constant use of the Liquor either simple or diluted, hath been found by long experience to avail much to health and long life; preserving the drinkers of it in their full strength and vigour even to very old Age." So reported John Worlidge in his 'Treatise of Cider' published in 1676. We even hear of one landlord who refused to grant life-tenancies to cider-drinkers! When King Charles I visited Hereford during the Civil War, he found consolation for his woes in the local ciders and in 1664 John Evelyn wrote -

> "
> *Ambrosial fruit and nectareous juice. . . .*
> *The Redstreak as supreme,*
> *While pulpous fruit, with gold,*
> *Irradiate and vermilion shines.*
> "
>
> FROM JOHN PHILLIPS

"**Generally all strong and pleasant cyder excites and cleanses the stomach, strengthens digestion and infallibly frees the kidneys and bladder from breeding the Gravel Stone.**" Strong medicine indeed! In fact, with its high acidity it was probably a great deal safer to drink than a lot of the Hereford water. Cider has always excited the imagination of poets and ballad writers alike, from John Philips 1,456 line extolment of 1708 - to the more down-to-earth -

> "But hard cider as much as you please
> Loose your teeth and bow your knees,
> Sour your gut and make you wheeze
> Thin your blood and kill your fleas,
> Hard cider as much as you please."

Amongst the hundreds of Cider Apple varieties, many sadly now extinct, the Redstreak must reign supreme. Developed by the first Viscount Scudamore on his Holme Lacy estate before the Civil War and the father of most modern fruit, it gave its name to the Red-Streak Tree Inn which until 1810, stood on the site of the present Butter Market. Worlidge said that *"The Redstreak was to be preferred for your Plantation to any other apple whatsoever especially remote from your House. First, because it yields the best of British Drinks. Secondly, because the Fruit is harsh and unpleasant, not tempting the Palates of lewd Persons."*

Not quite what Philips wrote perhaps! Other evocatively named varieties were 'Ten Commandments', 'Slack-my-girdle', 'Yellow Musk' and 'Gennet Moyle' mentioned in the 13th century and still grown today, one tree at least being known of in Herefordshire.

STRAINING THE CYDER.

PRESSING THE CHEESE.

Although Hereford and Cider have always been synonymous, the great heyday of Cidermaking came during the latter half of the 17th century when "The Hereford orchards were a pattern for all England" and cider and perry were in high repute. Francis Bacon found it "A wonderful and refreshing drink" and it was often described as the wine of England, standing comparison with many wines from the Continent.

During the 18th century cider entered upon a slow decline. Various factors responsible included increased corn growing, the distillation of grain and consequent demand for cheap gin, followed by heavy taxation and Government propaganda to encourage the drinking of beer. By the middle of the century, wine began to flow in from the Continent as the wars became intermittent and the wealthier classes turned from the apple to the grape. On Herefordshire farms, cider continued to be consumed in vast quantities, particularly at haymaking and harvest. It was customary to pay farm workers about a fifth of their wages in cider, known as 'Truck' and two gallon a day men were far from uncommon!

Surplus cider produced was bought by so-called 'Middlemen', who sold it on to merchants in London and Bristol who in turn exported it all over the world. Middlemen were often suspected of adulterating bad cider to make it sweeter and more drinkable, although they were not the only culprits. The 'Retail Compounder and Publican's Friend' of 1794 offers the following advice - "To Sophisticate Cider - For want of richness, add sugar of lead. For flavour, oak chips. For excess of sourness, Plaster of Paris or chalk." A recipe for 'English Port' from the 'Innkeeper's and Butler's Guide' in 1805 starts - "Take 40 gallons of good cider"!!!   ▷

'THE CIDER MILL', PAINTING BY HENRY ZIEGLER C. 1850.

With the advent of the Napoleonic Wars, the supply of imported wine dried up, interest in cider revived and consumption increased. The price of 'Common Cider' was fixed at a meeting of dealers at Hereford Fair on the 20th October annually and in 1805 varied from £1-5-0 to 2 guineas per hogshead (110 galls). Transportation was always a terrible problem. Local roads were impassable for most of the year and the river Wye was the only other way out of the County. Even so, barges often waited for up to six weeks at Hereford for enough water to pull down to Chepstow and Bristol.

Pioneer horticulturalist Thomas Andrew Knight of Downton Castle was the first to systematically develop new apple varieties and in 1811, he produced the wonderful illustrated work describing cider apples and perry pears, 'Pomona Herefordiensis', now one of the many interesting exhibits displayed in the Cider Museum just outside the city centre.

Again there was a slump in cidermaking in Herefordshire and it was not until the arrival of the canal in 1845, closely followed by the railway eight years later that cider production began on a commercial scale. Gradually the trend moved from farm to factory and in 1867 the names of William Evans and Joseph Boulton are listed as Hereford Cidermakers, later to be joined by the Watkins Pomona Cider company as well as several smaller concerns.

1887 was an important milestone in the long history of Hereford cider, for it was then that Percy Bulmer left his father's rectory at Credenhill to set up business in the city, where he was soon joined by his brother Fred and together they formed H. P. Bulmer and Company. From these modest beginnings 100 years ago Bulmers have grown into the United Kingdom's largest cider producer and now the only cidermakers in the city of Hereford. In their factory, 1,000 tons of apples can be processed per day and at their Moorfields site is the largest vessel in the world for storing alcholic liquor; a steel storage tank holding over 1.6 million gallons - a far cry indeed from the 18th century when this would have represented the annual cider production of the whole of Herefordshire. □

THE CHANGING TIMES

CHARLES ANTHONY, FOUNDER AND FIRST EDITOR OF THE HEREFORD TIMES AND SIX TIMES MAYOR OF HEREFORD.

THE HEREFORD TIMES OFFICES IN MAYLORD STREET IN 1858.

For 157 years The Hereford Times has been the mirror in which the life of the city and county has been reflected. Through its columns its readers have shared the triumphs and tragedies as well as the hundreds of other news items which are the bread and butter of a community newspaper.

The newspaper was born on 30th June, 1832, in a period when Hereford - then with a population of 10,000 - and the country were ripe for change. It was the time of the Reform Bills, the beginning of the ordinary man and woman's awakening to social injustice, of growing resentment at the sharp contrasts between rich and poor.

There were demands for the vote for all - few people had this right - and political corruption was commonplace.

In Hereford itself, town modernisation was long overdue. The death rate was high, higher even than London, through lack of proper sewers and water supplies.

It was against this backcloth that Charles Anthony, at the age of 29, launched his newspaper - The Hereford Times and embarked on a path which was to see him achieve not only business success but also a remarkable contribution to the city.

His father was manager of the Hereford branch of a family cloth manufacturing company, to which Charles was apprenticed at the age of 13, after education at a private school in Holmer. His father died when he was 16, and by the time he was 25 Charles himself had become manager.

An interest in writing and social causes was developing, and he was a regular contributor to the Conservative Hereford Journal, the established local newspaper dating back to 1713. Eventually the twin lures of print and politics won the day. Charles Anthony sold his interest in the cloth firm, gave up his job and founded

The Hereford Times as a Liberal newspaper dedicated, as his prospectus proclaimed, to "the Elucidation of the truth". That first newspaper - a four-page broadsheet - cost a staggering 7d, the equivalent in today's terms of about £1.40. Four pence of the cover price was a Government tax - the notorious "tax on knowledge" eventually to be repealed by Gladstone in 1862. The price later came down as low as 1½d. It is ironic that in 1989 the Government is again contemplating a tax - an extension of VAT - which could affect "the public prints" and make information less accessible to many less well-off people!

His newspaper up and running, Charles turned his attention to civic affairs, joining the town council in 1836. It was the start of a distinguished civic career. He was Mayor six times - a record, an alderman, a JP and a trustee of various municipal charities.

In those early years, using his position as owner-editor of the newspaper to back his social beliefs and causes, he promoted the Hereford Improvement Act which led to the building of new town sewers, a water works, a gas works, the cattle and butter markets and the extension of the railway lines to Hereford from Newport and Shrewsbury.

Charles Anthony did a great deal for Hereford, not least in establishing an alternative newspaper. Married three times, with two sons and two daughters by his second wife, Ann, he died in 1885, aged 81, having handed over the editorship to Charles junior in 1876. His funeral report, in his own paper, says something about the stature of the man. The procession of carriages was half-mile long and seven thousand citizens turned out to pay a final tribute.

Charles junior and his brother Edwyn, a barrister, inherited the Times and traded as Anthony Bros. - Charles editing, Edwyn looking after the commercial side.

The Anthony connection lasted for 77 years, until 1910, when financial difficulties arose. In that year the newspaper was sold, saved in fact by a local rescue consortium headed by Sir Anthony Croft, of Croft Castle. Professional management was brought in in the form of a new editor/manager, journalist and barrister Saxon Mills. One effect the new order had was a political switch - the paper went Conservative.

Two years later, order restored, Mills moved on and handed over to C.J. Bex. In 1922 he was succeeded by George Peacock, who was followed in 1949 by

his son Philip - to mark up a 48-year father and son occupation of the editor's chair. Once again the move saw a change of political stance, George Peacock adopting the independent position which has continued ever since.

The ownership changed again in 1927 when the consortium sold to the Macaskie family, who had local newspaper interests in London.

A major milestone was passed in 1932 - the newspaper's centenary year - when it bought and absorbed its older rival, the Hereford Journal.

After proprietor George Mackaskie's death in 1963 Berrow's Newspaper Ltd. - publishers of the Hereford Evening News and the Hereford Citizen and Bulletin - bought The Hereford Times. Soon afterwards its came for the first time under a major group, as Berrow's itself was acquired by Rupert Murdoch's News International.

The Times then moved from its old Maylord Street base to Berrow's printing centre in Bath Street - absorbing the Citizen and Bulletin on the way.

There was a change in the editorship in 1970, when Philip Peacock retired and was succeeded by Ray Goulding, a major influence in setting the newspaper on course for the future. He was succeeded in 1973 by the present editor, Richard Shields.

Another ownership change came in 1982, when Murdoch sold the Berrows's Group to Reed International. Now retitled Reed Midland Newspapers, the group is part of a major publishing empire, though by deliberate policy each newspaper retains a high degree of autonomy and local responsibility for its own destiny.

For the present Hereford Times management team and staff, based in Aubrey Street, this means both freedom and responsibility. Freedom to use their professional skills to produce the best possible newspaper for their community, always following the philosophy expressed at the beginning by the founder as "the elucidation of the truth". Responsibility, rightly, to readers and to shareholders.

The Hereford Times of 1989 - running at a record circulation level of more than 37,500 copies per week, and with more pages than ever before - is in good health.

And, in its 157th year, it is still what Charles Anthony intended - a grassroots, community newspaper. We like to think that if he were alive today he might perhaps be pleased at his creation's progress.   □

FREEMEN OF THE CITY

17TH CENTURY PEWTER TANKARDS, PART OF THE CITY'S COLLECTION OF PLATE & PEWTER.

"In all the things and above all things you must take great heed not to be forsworn in anything because the custom of the City is, if a man be convicted of perjury he shall lose his freedom and never recover it again unless by the special favour of the commonalty and by the redemption of your goods and chattels for at least twice as much as you gave before. You are charged that you must have some tenements or yearly revenues upon the Queen's fee within a year and a day next following by which you may justify yourself unto the Queen and Her commonalty. If you have not you shall lose your freedom. You must be prepared as well by day as by night armed with weapons fitting to your degree, whenever you shall be warned by the Mayor or hear the ringing of our common bell for the tuition of the City or the tranquillity of the citizens abiding in the same. You shall not quit from toll or murage or any other customs of the City of of any other City or villages unless you be staying and abiding amongst us, uprising and down-lying."

Thus runs the ancient Freemen's charge which in its ancient archaic language has been administered to holders of that office, whether on a hereditary or honorary basis, over the years. "Tuition" as Latin scholars will appreciate is used in its original meaning of "guardianship" and "murage" was a tax for the building and upkeep of town-walls. The common bell referred to had a twofold purpose firstly that after its ringing any "vagabonds or night walkers" in the City or suburbs were liable to be incarcerated overnight at the pleasure of the Chief Bailiff (the predecessor in title of our present day Mayor). Secondly it served the important function of warning of catastrophe befalling the City such as a major fire, civil strife, sedition or enemies approaching the city. If a freeman did not answer the call to arms in such circumstances he was accounted a rebel and a perjured person. These days it is assumed that the common bell is that of St. Peters traditionally the "Town Hall Church".

The rights and privileges which freemen used to enjoy have largely fallen into desuetude and the creation of freemen in recent years has been the result of the Council passing a resolution pursuant to section 249 of the Local Government Act, 1972. This permits local authorities which have City or borough status (Hereford has both as a result of charters granted by the Queen at the time of local government reorganisation) to hold a specially covered meeting with, as the Act puts it "notice of the object" at which if two-thirds of the members present vote for the resolution "persons of distinction and persons who have, in the opinion of the Council, rendered eminent services to the City" can be admitted to be honorary freemen of the City. The passing of the resolution is the moment when the freedom is created but there is usually some time later a formal ceremony when, with due pomp, a casket, historically made of apple wood, containing an illuminated address (normally a suitably decorated copy of the resolution) is presented to the newly created freeman. It should be noted that freedoms can be granted to those who have no direct connection with the City and among past recipients are Lord Nelson and the former Poet Laureate John Masefield. The most recently created freemen have tended to be members (and occasionally officers) who have served the Council diligently over many years but, given that a freedom is the highest honour of dignity that it is the City's privilege to bestow, the tradition has been maintained of widening the ranks of the freemen in that, for instance one of the present living freemen is the noted explorer Colonel John Nicholas Blashford-Snell, MBE.,   □

Horse Trading to Hi-Tech

MAYLORD ORCHARDS 1989

We are very proud of our heritage in Hereford; it being built up on a genuine and reliable business foundation. Although originally founded on an agricultural economy as a true county market city in the centre of its shire, surrounded by satellite towns, Hereford has moved with the times - coming to terms with, and exploiting, the advent of canals, railways, cars and high-tech communications.

Trade and commerce in Hereford was the back-bone of the City's development prior to tourism, with a number of well-respected local families building up their own business enterprises, and at the same time persuading other associated trades to join them and further expand trade in our marvellous City.

Over the centuries Hereford has always been a market and trading centre from which to buy and sell, and this trading continues in the modern City. It has been a magnet because of its agricultural background, drawing many thousands from this predominantly agricultural area to its centre, and this catchment has been greatly extended over recent years and is now well beyond the County limits, encroaching into the old County of Worcestershire, Gloucestershire, the South West and Central Wales, as well as Shropshire. The mix of farming, industry, commerce, professions, tourists and traders gives the City a diversity of interest and vitality that belies its small town image, and creates on busy days an atmosphere of prosperity and purpose quite unusual for a place of

its size. Where else can you find a better place to conduct your business, at the same time viewing the sites, enjoying the river, refreshing yourselves in the numerous eating and drinking establishments, thus making yourself ready for the journey home?

At the heart of our City lies High Town, one of the first traffic-free areas in the Country, and now added to by Eign Gate, Commercial Street, and our highly acclaimed and award-winning Maylord Orchards Shopping Centre. This Centre, developed by the Norwich Union Insurance Group in connection with our City Council, is designed to meet the increasing demands placed by both shoppers and retailers alike, and is a MUST for all visitors, as is our Cathedral, Market Hall, Livestock and Retail Market, the New Leisure Centre, and the many other Tourist attractions. With this outstanding background of family tradition and the expansion that the City Fathers have so jealously guarded, the possibility of our outer Ring Road to relieve the inner one, the continued expansion of our leading employers, namely H.P. Bulmer and Sun Valley Poultry, and the ever increasing requirement for more industry, out future surely is assured! Hereford & District Chamber of

Commerce is confident that we can progress into the future, take up the challenge of the Common Market and expect to increase and strengthen our role in business activities in the immediate area and beyond. An enlarging City, and expanding economy, which is embraced within a consumer conscious framework, can only bring benefits to the whole community - clients, employers, workers, residents and visitors to this beautiful part of the Country.

The Chamber of commerce fights tirelessly to enhance business opportunities in the City and all looks well in its 800th Anniversary Year with the proposed partnership with its neighbouring Counties' Chambers, to form an ever stronger and more vibrant team to herald the 2000's.   □

MAYLORD ORCHARDS 1989

A Centre for Agricultural Marketing

Any publication tracing the history of Hereford would be incomplete without reference to the importance of agriculture in the development of the city.

Hereford is situated in one of the most fertile counties in England and because of this, agriculture and the marketing of agricultrual products has had considerable influence on the city, right up to the present day, and many of the leading commercial enterprises, notably Bulmers and Sun Valley Poultry, are agricultural based companies.

Originally the marketing of agricultural produce took place in the streets of the town at two great Annual Fairs held in May and October of each year and for which royal permission was granted by King Henry II to the Bishop of the diocese in 1227. These fairs continued through the centuries until in the 1840's, pressure began to mount in the town to remove the livestock from the streets to purpose built premises, and on the 17th October 1856, Hereford's brand new municipal stock market was opened on its present site.

At this time, Hereford was considered one of the leading provincial markets in the country and over the course of the next 120 years, proceeded to consolidate this position, particularly in the 1950's when a major modernisation scheme made Hereford one of the largest and most up-to-date stock markets in the country.

The importance of this scheme to the City was reflected in the presence of her Royal Highness Queen Elizabeth II at the opening ceremony.

In 1989 the Cattle Market is still an important feature in the commercial life of the City. Gone are the days when sales were limited to the two great fair days, the market now operates regularly four days a week and attracts stock from a vast catchment area. Purchasers from all over the country attend the market, which has gained a formidable reputation for the quality and quantity of livestock on offer. The total throughput in 1988 amounted to almost half a million head of cattle, sheep and pigs, with a value in excess of forty three million pounds.

In recent years there have been many changes, gone are the days when two thousand red and white Hereford cattle can be seen on one day. The introduction of continental breeds and the swing from beef to sheep production caused by the common agricultural policy, have reduced cattle throughputs and produced a variety of breeds on offer which never used to exist. Sheep numbers continue to grow to such an extent that buildings which a few years ago were full to capacity for only a few weeks of the year, are overflowing almost every week. There are other changes to be seen, computers now do the work that used to occupy numerous clerks for many hours. The site buzzes on Wednesdays and Saturdays to the sound of market traders selling everything from fruit and vegetables to clothes and footwear. Through the summer months a flood of tourists and day trippers invade the site, keen to savour the atmosphere and flavour of a traditional livestock market and hear the intriguing sound of the auctioneer at work.

In addition to the regular sales commercial livestock, the market has lor been the centre for Pedigree Beef Catt sales, most notably on behalof of tl Hereford Herdbook Society.

The Hereford breed dominated the wor beef industry for almost a 100 years ar the cattle market at Hereford gained international reputation for its Herefo breed sales. Although the introduction continental breeds in the late 1960s ar 1970s reduced the popularity of tl Hereford, these sales still attract buye from all over the world and indeed recent years demand for the Herefo has begun to grow again.

The marketing of livestock and oth agricultural products has done much enhance the reputation of Hereford bo nationally and internationally over tl years and with the advent of the op market in 1992 thoroughout Europe, is to be hoped that the City's livesto market will continue to develop ar further enhance the reputation of our cit

THE CATTLEMARKET C. 1900

FAMILY HISTORY

In years gone by it was called Genealogy and conducted by an academic few in hushed and hallowed surroundings, with rather a restricted access to many documents.

Today it is called Family History, a pastime or all-consuming hobby, followed and enjoyed by an ever-increasing number of people in all ranks of life. There is a Family History Society within virtually every county of England and Wales, and sometimes more than one. There are others, such as the One Name Societies, designed to bring together information from all those people working on the same surname.

The Herefordshire Family History Society was formed in March 1980 and meets every month at St. Paul's School, Tupsley. Beginners are always welcome and are sure of any help that they may need to start them on their way. There is usually a talk on some aspect of family history designed to help us in our researched, or illustrate what life was like 100 or 200 years ago.

There is now a multitude of books and inexpensive booklets, not only on how to begin your family history but also on how to locate the various types of records that are useful or necessary as one progresses.

Family History means, or should mean, just that - and not just a bare chart of ancestors showing births, marriages and deaths. What a nice conversation - piece to find that your greatgreatgrand-father was described as a mole-catcher, and that he had 'graduated' to that position from a humble agricultural labourer.

Admittedly one needs the framework to hang any other details on, and the first stage is to consult the Civil Registration records which began in 1837. Until quite recently this normally meant a trip to London to look through the country-wide indexes of births, marriages and deaths, but these indexes have now been microfilmed and are viewable in other localities. The indexes for 1837 to 1865 are available at our local Record Office in Harold Street, and it is hoped that later years will be added soon. ▷

CHILDREN OF THE HATTON FAMILY, NEAR THE VICTORIA BRIDGE C. 1899

▷ When one gets back to over 100 years ago it is possible to use the census returns made every 10 years and available on microfilm at the Record Office. I defy anyone not to experience a thrill on finding their grandfather at the tender age of 4 or 5, listed along with his parents and brothers and sisters on the night of the census. Also shown is everyone's occupation, age, and where they were born, which can be very useful when one reaches the time before 1837 and parish registers have to be used. Most of the latter have been deposited at the Record Office and can be seen on microfilm At this stage, what extra information to be gleaned from the entries depends on the whim of the incumbent. In most cases ther is just the bare detail:

'27th October 1791, Baptism of William, son of William Scattergood by Martha his wife.'

In all too few cases there is a bit of extra information:

'13th April 1728 Baptism of Anne daughter of William Thomas of Evenjobb banke an honest poor labouring carpenter by Mary his wife.'

As parish registers have been kept since 1538 it is theoretically possible to trace ones ancestors back to that time, but in practice this is highly unlikely as many of the early registers have been lost, usually during the Commonwealth period. Depending upon the mobility of one's ancestors it would be more realistic to expect to reach 1660, although further positive progress is possible if the family in question were in the habit of making wills.

These are often a fascinating and useful source of information, as the members of the family are often mentioned together with the legacy they are to receive . Early wills often have an inventory of the testator's possessions, which can provide a clue as to his occupation and standing.

Other sources of information await the eager researcher- -marriage licences, tithe maps, land tax lists etc, etc.

And not to be ignored are our local papers which can provide you with a bonus. What can be made of the advertisement of June 1887, put in the Hereford Times by my greatgrandfather? - 'I hereby give notice that I will not be answerable for any debts incurred by my wife after this date.' □

PARKER'S STEAMER AT BELMONT, 2ND JULY 1894, MEMBERS OF THE HATTON FAMILY TEA.

CITY OF HEREFORD

CITY OF HEREFORD TOURIST INFORMATION CENTRE
Town Hall, St Owens Street, Hereford HR1 2PJ. Telephone (0432) 268430
To find out what's on in Hereford call
INFOLINE Hereford 277000

charities

"The City of Hereford can perhaps boast of more public charities than any other place of similar extent in the kingdom". This was a comment in The Hereford Times of 1839. It was a reflection of the destitution which had been prevalent in Hereford after the closure of the monasteries by Henry VIII and the decline of the wollen trade when fulling mills were closed at the same time. The enforcement of the Elizabethan Poor Laws meant harsh treatment for vagrants and the plight of the 'deserving poor' was acute. Some of the old medieval hospitals remained: **ST. ETHELBERT'S (1225)** and newly rebuilt in 1805 in Castle Street for 'decayed gentlewomen', **ST. GILES (1290)** in St. Owen's Street, and **LAZAR'S** or Sickmens', founded when leprosy was common.

After the 1601 Poor Law Act, money was donated in wills to found sheltered accommodation of "alms" houses. Bread had been supplied to the poor by the Canons' Bakehouse which was by the Castle Street entrance to the cathedral and dole money was also left for this purpose, **WILLIAMS HOSPITAL** was built near St. Giles in 1601 and a chapel was added for both sets of inmates in 1682 and still stands in St. Owen Street. Six aged men and their families were accommodated. No longer standing, **LINGEN HOSPITAL (1609)** was founded by Mrs. Jane Shelley for six poor widows. It has now been replaced in Whitecross Road by modern housing. The most interesting one founded in 1614 is **CONINGSBY HOSPITAL** in Widemarsh Street. This is said to have been the model for the Chelsea Hospital. Here "worn out" veterans and servants were housed in buildings on a site which had belonged to the Knights of St. John. Part of their medieval hall and chapel remain and may be visited.

A uniform was supplied and that of the Chelsea Pensioners resembles it. The accommodation here has recently been modernised.

The most picturesque almshouses still in use are those in Berrington Street known as **AUBREY'S ALMS-HOUSES.** These timber-framed buildings date from 1630 when Mrs. Mary Price left a bequest for poor widows and single women. They are still in use. **PRICE'S ALMSHOUSES (1665)** were rebuilt after the Civil War when conditions worsened. They are still in use with their chapel as an integral part of the stone building in Whitecross Road. Many houses have vanished and include Weavers', Symonds' Hospital, Trinity Hospital and Trehearnes'

Of more recent date are:
Roberts' Almshouses (1930)
St. Owen's and Emma Cams (1932)
Caroline Thompson (1933)
Bricknell Webb Almshouses (1968)
Lindsey Price (1984)
Millar Almshouses (1986) ▷

LAURDRY, WORKING BOYS HOME IN BATH STREET IN 1891.

Many of the almshouses and funds are administered today by the trustees of the Municipal Charities who receive applications for accommodation.

The New Poor Law of 1836 did little to relieve the acute distress of the poor in the 1840's and many people were frightened of the new workhouses. The vicar of St. Peter's, the Rev. John Venn, founded the Society for Aiding the Industrious in 1841. This began with a soup distribution to feed the hungry; then cheap coal and loans were provided. the great innovation was a money-making steam mill to grind corn for the poor.

It made a fortune and from the proceeds other enterprises were started. By John Venn's death in 1890 the Society had become incorporated and owned much property. His vision ensured the welfare of the "deserving poor" for over a hundred years. In 1936 the **VENN'S CLOSE** of houses were built by the Society which it still administers. The mill was working through World War II and although it has been converted into shops it still stands in Bath Street as a memorial next to the baths which it heated and where many Hereford schoolchildren of the past leaned to swim.

Today Herefordians band together to raise money for charity and their generosity has resulted in many appeals being met. Modern hospitals are concerned to fight illness and help the handicapped while municipal sheltered-housing has diminished the need for individuals to found almshouses but poverty, although not extreme, still exists. □

A CITY OF MUSEUMS

With eight varied and interesting Museums to explore, Hereford is able to provide many glimpses of the past, from mosiac pavements and pictures, to costume and uniforms, steam and cider - truly something for everyone.

▽

CITY MUSEUM AND ART GALLERY, BROAD STREET.

Displays illustrating the natural and early history of Hereford and its environs can be seen together with interesting craft and folklore material. Bee-keeping displays include an observation hive and photographs by Alfred Watkins, whose camera and photographic inventions are also on show. Roman life at Kenchester and that of Iron Age tribesmen are reflected in the Archaeological displays. The Art Gallery has important collections of early 19th Century watercolours, and the works of modern artists and local painters are well represented. There are changing exhibitions each month. A well stocked Museum shop sells catalogues, guides, cards and gifts.

THE BULMER RAILWAY CENTRE
STANDARD GUAGE STEAM RAILWAY MUSEUM

The Centre, opened in 1968, houses the famous GWR locomotive 'King George V' following its restoration by H.P. Bulmer Ltd. It later bacame the home of two other restored locomotives, LMS 'Princess Elizabeth' and SR 'Clan Line'. As working engines, however, they can be occasionally absent on main line operations elsewhere. The Centre also houses a collection of industrial locomotives and rolling stock.

HEREFORDSHIRE REGIMENTAL MUSEUM, HAROLD STREET.

Housed at the TA Centre is this excellent military museum. Its fascinating collection of uniforms, colours, weapons and documents can be seen together with medals and regimental silver. One of the most interesting exhibits is the flag of Admiral Doenitz, the last Fuhrer of the Third Reich.

Whatever your interest, Hereford has something fascinating to offer you.

CHURCHILL GARDENS MUSEUM AND HATTON GALLERY, VENNS LANE, AYLESTONE HILL

Set in a large park on the City outskirts, the Museum features displays of fine furniture costume, paintings of the 18th and 19th Centuries together with a Victorian nursery, butler's pantry and parlour. The Sandford collection, a unique room of straw work and corn dollies will delight children and adults alike. The fine costume collection dated from 1700 to the present day also includes Queen Anne's hat, fine 18th and 19th Century silk dresses, and a large representative collection of local smocks. Special displays include barometers, local clocks and dolls. On the first floor a Victorian kitchen is in preparation.

CIDER MUSEUM
POMONA PLACE, GRIMMER ROAD.

The Cider Museum is housed in a former cider works and tells the fascinating story of traditional cider making through the ages, how apples were harvested, milled and pressed on the farm, right through to the mechanical production of Cider factories. The displays include an enormous 17th Century French beam press and a French travelling cider brandy still, together with travelling cidermaker's "tack", a Cooper's shop, original Champagne cider cellars, great oak vats of the Napoleonic period, 1920's hydraulic presses and factory bottling line. The Cider Brandy Distillery is the first to be licensed in Britain for over 250 years. The exciting Museum gift shop and off-licence sells a full range of distillery products together with locally made cider and perry. The Cider Museum is run by an independent Charitable Trust and is non-profit making. It is conveniently situated close to the City Centre, is entirely under cover and centrally heated with ample free car and coach parking.

THE OLD HOUSE, HIGH TOWN.

This fine Jacobean house, built in 1621 and once part of Butchers Row, is furnished on three floors with 17th Century furniture. The kitchen, hall and bedrooms with four-poster beds, can be seen together with the dog door in the master bedroom. Fine wall paintings and rich oak furniture are well worth examination. The Museum shop has a good selection of guides and souvenirs.

THE BROOMY HILL ENGINES
HEREFORDSHIRE WATERWORKS MUSEUM

This intriguing Museum features Victorian pumping engines and other exhibits, many of which can be operated by visitors. Located in a 19th Century pumping station next to the River Wye it is less than a mile from Hereford Cathedral.

ST. JOHN MEDIEVAL MUSEUM
CONINGSBY HOSPITAL, WIDEMARSH STREET.

This Museum is part of Coningsby Hospital and dates from the 13th Century. It includes the Chapel of the Knights Hospitaller of St. John of Jerusalem. In the floor is a skeleton thought to be that of a 15th Century Abbott. Models of Coningsby pensioners who used the hospital are on display in period dress, together with armour, blazons and exhibits depicting the fascinating history of the ancient Order of St. John during the 300 years of the Crusades. Coningsby Hospital itself was founded in 1614 by Sir Thomas Coningsby. Built as a quadrangle, which now includes the Museum, it originally comprised of 13 houses, a chapel, dining hall and infirmary. The almshouses are still in use today. Next to the hospital are the remains of BLACKFRIARS MONASTERY which together with the church, can be traced back to 1322, King Edward 111 and his son the Black Prince attended its consecration. The King's Confessor, the Bishop of Chester, died while in Hereford and was buried in the choir. After the dissolution, the monastery was eventually purchased by Sir Thomas Coningsby and all that remains today is the nave west of the cloister and the PREACHING CROSS. This 14th century cross, one of few surviving examples in England, has recently been restored. The tranquil ruins are now set in a delightful rose garden. ☐

THE PUBLIC LIBRARY SERVICE

The adoption of the Public Libraries Act of 1865 by the citizens of Hereford in 1871 heralded the first library in the city to be freely available to all and to be rate-supported. The foundation and provision of the present building opened in 1874 in Broad Street are owed to the generosity of Sir James Rankin of Bryngwyn. He had been enthusiastic as a member and then as president of the Woolhope Club in his aim to establish to a museum in association with a free library and provided the necessary money for land and building. While the building was being erected, the library occupied temporary premises at 3 King Street. Among the first books to be made available were those pruchased from a grant from the Penny Readings Fund which had come into existence in 1864. The libraries of St. Peter's Literary Institution and Hereford Working Men's Institution were subsequently acquired.

Up to 1912 books were in closed access and were selected by reference to the catalogue. The growth of the library relied heavily on donations of books and money. Improvements by way of some extensions to the building were made during the 1890's including the opening of a reading room for women. At the turn of the century a reference library was established and through bequests made by Sir Joseph Pulley of Eaton Bishop and his nephew Charles the large extension on the west side was completed in 1912.

In 1915 the city was fortunate to receive by way of bequest the important collections of Walter Pilley, the local antiquary. His library remains intact today, stored in the strongroom at Broad Street.

The 1920's and 1930's saw considerable progress in the development of the library. The Dewey decimal classification was adopted and various grants were received to upgrade the accommodation. By 1945 the library's reputation had been greatly enhanced, particularly by the consolidation of a comprehensive Herefordshire local studies collection. By 1974 major remodelling of the interior had been achieved by the insertion of a mezzanine floor. When the City lost its library powers under the Local Government Act of 1972, all that was possible had been done to extend the library within the confines of the original premises.

In the late 1930's the former Herefordshire County Council, having adopted the Public Libraries Act of 1919 in 1926, established a lending library at its offices in Bath Street for county residents and students. This transferred to the old Garrick Theatre in Widemarsh Street in 1946 where it closed in 1974 when the new Hereford and Worcester County Libraries system was established under local government reorganisation. The public services were then concentrated at Broad Street with administrative support housed elsewhere in the city.

The LEA has made its college libraries accessible to the public and reference must be made to the former Hereford College of Education, which closed in 1978, and to the Herefordshire Technical College and the Herefordshire College of Art and Design, whose libraries were amalgamated in 1988 to form the new Herefordshire Campus Library.

The need for a new central library in Hereford has long been acknowledged and is now urgent if the community is to enjoy to full advantage all the benefits available through an up-to-date library service, whose purpose is to provide access to books and other appropriate media to meet the educational, cultural, recreational and information needs of all. ☐

HEREFORD LIBRARY IN THE 1930'S.

HEREFORD'S MILITARY TRADITION

FIRST REGIMENTAL CAMP 1871 AT BROONY HILL.

The HRVC provided Volunteer Service Companies who went out to South Africa and fought with the 2nd Bn KSLI. For this service the battle honour South Africa 1900 - 1902 is borne on the Regimental Colour.

The 1st Battalion, the Herefordshire Regiment, served with distinction in the Great War 1914 - 1918. They landed at Suvla Bay during the Gallipoli Campaign and then went to Egypt and took part in the Palestine Campaign with Allenby, entering Jerusalem in December, 1917 and on to Tel Azur. The Battalion then returned to France in 1918 and joined 34 Division between Chateau Thierry and Soissons. For its war service, the Regiment was awarded 16 Battle Honours, 10 of which are emblazoned on the Queen's Colour.

The 1st Battalion, The Herefordshire Regiment (TA) were mobilised again on 2nd September,1939 as part of 53 Welsh Infantry Division, and after service in Northern Ireland, moved with 159 Infantry Brigade to join 11th Armoured Division. They landed in Normandy on D Day and after the fierce battles at Odon and Caen, the Division broke out at Caumont and took part in the battles at Falaise and the advance to Antwerp. Then came the winter battles of the Maas and the Rhine crossing, then the drive to the Baltic, ending the war with the capture of Admiral Doenitz and his puppet Government at Flensburg on 23rd May, 1945.

When the TA re-formed after the war, the Herefordshire Regiment was reconstituted as the Herefordshire Light Infantry, part of the corps of the KSLI. With the re-organisation and reduction of the TA in 1966, the County lost its own Battalion and retained two companies, one at Hereford and one at Ross as part of the 5th Bn. The Light Infantry, with the Bn HQ at Shrewsbury

With the development of the Rifle Voluneer Corps in Herefordshire, the Armoury and drill hall were set up in Friar's Street and the Battalion HQ was at 20 St. Owen Street, the Castle Green being used for training and drills. When training camps were authorised, the HRVC went into camp for the first time at Broomy Hill in 1871. In 1890, local camps were discontinued and units attended Brigade Camps at a distance. The Hereford Battalion joined the Welsh Border Brigade for its camp at Towyn in 1890.

Many different elements make up the Military History of Herefordshire at varying periods, and Hereford has had its full share of participation in these forces, with a very rich martial heritage from the Border wars onwards.

Names still of memory and repute in the County are found constantly recurring down the long scroll of territorial fame. Crofts, Lingens, Blounts, Scudamore, Bodenham, Wigmores, Vaughans, Harleys, Barnebys, Kyrles, Dunnes, Carless and Haywood.

From 1701 to 1881, Herefordshire had its own Regular Regiment, the 36th Regiment of Foot, but with successive Army Reforms and reductions, this merged into the Worcestershire Regiment.

The Herefordshire Militia, which had its roots in the old Shire Levies of 1539, was regimented in 1788. In 1881, it became the 4th Militia Bn The Kings Shropshire Light Infantry and was disbanded in 1908 with the organisation of the Territorial Force.

The Volunteer Cavalry and Infantry were entirely separate from the Militia and were first raised as independent Corps in the 1790's and disbanded after Waterloo. The continous history of Herefordshire Regiment starts in 1860 with the formation of the Rifle Volunteers, which became the 1st Herefordshire Rifle Corps in 1880 and the 1st Battalion The Herefordshire Regiment in 1908 with the formation of the Territorial Force.

▷

▷ During 1890, the Herefordshire Militia had established their HQ and Armoury at Harold Street, Hereford were they also had their drill ground. With the formation of the Territorial Force in 1908 and the disbandment of the Militia, the new Territorial Battalion, The Herefordshire Regiment, formed at Harold Street and the St. Owen Street property was given up. The builkding used at that time is now in use by the Record Office, and the successor units of The Light Infantry (TA) are housed in the Territorial Army Centre which was built 1959, adjacent to the old buildings. Located in the same building is the Museum of the Herefordshire Regiment/ Herefordshire Light Infantry.

HEREFORDSHIRE MILITIA PARADE, BROAD STREET 1883.

PERSONALITIES

In 1648, Charles, Prince of Wales, later Charles II, signed a commission to Sir Edward Hopton of Herefordshire, to raise a Regiment of Horse and a Regiment of Foot in Herefordshire, to fight the King's enemies. A successor to Sir Edward became a famous soldier, Lieut General Sir E. Hopton, KCB. His medals, the KCB, Indian Mutiny and Crimean Medals, are on display in the Regimental Museum, on loan from the City Museum.

In 1810, the Herefordshire Militia, under command of Sir John Cotterell, were reviewed on the banks of the Lugg by General Warde, who was well pleased. The Mayor of Hereford and Magistrates also expressed their satisfaction with the conduct of the Militia when embodied for training.

On 10th April, 1908, the last Commanding Officer of the Militia, Colonel Shipley, presented Hereford City Council with the Regimental Colours and Base Drum, and a number of pieces of silver. These items are held on display in the Town Hall, the Colours restored and framed in the Council Chamber.

Colonel Mackay J. G. Scobie, was commissioned into the HRVC in 1873 and commanded the Battalion from 1899 - 1908, becoming the first CO of the Herefordshire Regiment, commanding until 1911 when he became Honorary Colonel. He received Volunteer Decoration and the Terrtorial Decoration, and was made Commander of the BATA.

The HRVS were allowed a limited number of Volunteer to serve with the two volunteers Services Companies which went to serve with the 2nd Btn KSLI in the South African War. As the numbers were limited, Cpt. Rankin of Hereford VSC volunteered as an individual, and served with distinction with Rimingtons Horse. Pte. G. Cox, also of Hereford, was with 1st VSC and was in the leading section on 27th May, 1900 when 2nd KSLI marched across the Vaal River into the Transvaal.

Among personalities who served in the Great War 1914 - 18 were Major W.F. Chipp, who had been awarded the DSO, MC and the Croix de Guerre, and L/Sgt. J.B. Symonds, who won the DCM and MM.

In 1921, on the re-formation of the TA, the 1st Battalion The Herefordshire Regiment, was commanded by Lt. H.E.P. Pateshall, who had received the DSO, while serving with the Herefords in the Palestine campaign. He later became Honorary Colonel of the Regiment, and his medals are on display in the Regimental Museum at Harold Street.

In the 1939 - 45 War, Major Paul Barnsley received a DSO while serving with the 1/7th Queen's Regiment, and he later returned to the Herefordshire Regiment as a Company Commander, and then commanded a Home Guard Battalion. After the War, He ran a well - known estate agency in Hereford. The citation for his DSO is held in the Regimental Museum.

□

OLD MEMORIES OF HEREFORD

Much has been written about the Cathedral, the Old Wye Bridge, the Old House, the Castle Green, etc., but there are so many odd things to be found out in our City which are not in the guide books.

On the end wall of St. Giles Hospital in St. Owen Street will be found a Norman Tympanum carved with "A Christ in Majesty". It came from the Circular Church built for the Knights Templers nearby. When St. Giles Chapel was moved and rebuilt in 1927 the carving was, unfortunately, fastened up in the open and is now very weather-worn. It was carved by the same masons who worked at Shobdon, Kilpeck, Eardisley etc. A fine example of this scene is at Rowlestone.

For instance, the initials "T.P.C." can be seen over doorways and windows. They stand for Thomas and Philippa Coningsby, who built the Hospital. Over the archway leading to the gardens is a beautifully carved Coat of Arms, showing the three Coneys for Coningsby. Over the doorway into the dining hall is a small carving of the family Crest. On the North side of the Hall is the old Circular Staircase leading to the Infirmary. The steps are made of great bulks of oak, except the first one, which is of stone. Could this be because of flooding from the old Widemarsh?

It is not often known that the stone pillars and entablature on the street frontage marked the entrance to the Monastery at the back, which Coningsby turned into a Town House. They were restored by Kings, the monumental masons.

COMMERCIAL STREET IN 1908

MAY FAIR C. 1900

Just below in the street there used to be an iron water trough standing on cast iron "horses legs". It was provided for the hundreds of horses which passed that way pulling carts, waggons, traps etc. It was paid for by subscription.

At the Coningsby Street end of the Old Graveyard, entered under the John Venn Archway in Commercial Road is another form of drinking trough, but this one was for humans. It was erected by Miss E. M. Wall in 1924.

There is no need now for such drinking fountains, everyone can afford a drink in the nearest pub!

Nearby, in the Coningsby Hospital there are interesting details to be found.

Many people are convinced that there are tunnels leading from the Cathedral in all directions. One is even marked on a map as running from 'Scots Hole', off Old Eign Hill; another is said to go from under the Bridge Street Arch of the Wye Bridge. There was an opening there, but it only led up to the wharf at the bottom of the street. Another was said to go from Coningsby Hospice. I have a letter from a man who says that when he was a boy, he tried to walk up the opening in the river bank under the Victoria Bridge believing it led to the Cathedral. But he retreated, covered in mud, when his lamp went out! This was where the Mill stream ran into the river (hence

Mill Street). As long as I can remember, this entrance was covered by a heavy flap, so I cannot see how he can even have started to walk up this "tunnel".

The truth is, every street in the City has been dug up at some time or other, and no one has ever come across one of these tunnels, and there are none. (Of course, if there is a Nunnery around, there are rumours of tunnels into it!)

Whilst walking along the pavements, one can be crossing history. There are a number of mediaeval cellars beneath your feet; in East Street a manhole cover near the front of the Conservative Club covered the terminal of the wires for the first telephone system in the City. It was run by "The National Telephone Company" around 1904. A Miss Kitty Lloyd was the sole operator.

Visitors often admire the carvings on the City Library in Broad Street, but there is nothing to tell them that the carvings were the work of Robert Clarke, the father of W.E.H. Clarke, the well-known architect in the City. He also carried out work on the Old House when it was restored in 1883.

Hereford City has more Societies and Charities to the square mile than any other town of its size. And, in the past, some strange ones. There was "The Society of Tempers" founded in 1752; it was instituted for the promotion of amiability and good ▷

GASLIT, HIGHTOWN 1890

BELOW
HIGHTOWN, MAYFAIR 1900.

◁ They met at the 'Bowling Green', perhaps it was a well it wasn't football they were playing. They later moved to the 'Swan and Falcon.' This was later to be the 'City Arms' now Barclays Bank. Such a Society would find plenty of scope today!

Boys were not so adventurous in my youth. By that I mean we were more afraid of people in authority. A visit to the Cathedral was a bit frightening, one dared hardly speak. I don't know what we expected to happen; maybe the vergers in their gowns were intimidating.

Fred" and a girl we always avoided, as she would suddenly lash out at one. Another 'card' was Mr. Cole. He was a good long distance runner and cyclist, but often wore a black track suit and had rather "staring" eyes; we were a bit nervous of him, especially the girls. Then there was one called "Mokey Hiles". He had an old pram and would be at the station and offer to carry your luggage on it.

But, of course, with the population more than double today, and hardly anyone without a car, one does not notice the individuals.

temper. The rules said members were "to bear and forbear, avoid personal and malicious reflections, to put no forced unkind or false interpretation on what is said or done".

There is a story about Alan Moore, the Head Verger for over fifty years. He was asked by an American visitor "Does anyone come to pray nowadays?" "Oh yes", he replied, "I caught one of them at it yesterday!"

Boys can be cruel to the afflicted, but there were more "characters" about in my young days. There was a man we called "Cherry". He lived at Madley, but always seemed to be pushing his bicycle, perhaps he rode it outside the town, but I am sorry to say we used to shout at him. Then there was "Batchy

Hereford City is crowded every day. Pre-war it was empty on a Thursday afternoon because of early closing - most of the shop assistants played football, there was even a team called "The Early Closers" and only really crowded on Wednesday, and at May Fair time.

And, thank Heavens, one never sees anyone in ragged clothes or no shoes, as one did only sixty years ago in certain parts of the town.   □

ALICK ROWE

— today and yesterday

HEREFORD BORE

"About Hereford - did you know?..."

There's excitement in my voice and eagerness but friends don't fool me with their polite interest, while others have been known to yawn as their eyes glaze over muttering "Here we go again."

It's a problem, living in an ancient place; the past keeps tapping you on the shoulder and the older you are the harder it taps. It's worse still if you grew up there. From my window I can see the street and the pub where I spent my childhood. Without particularly meaning to, I've come full circle. Perhaps people with roots on the Border have some kind of unexpected and invisible umbilical cord which extends about forty miles and turns us into pumpkins or something equally awkward to explain if we venture further.

In my childhood the past lay all around and had not yet been sanitised into Heritage. It was often untidy and unrecognised. I did not know that the rough patch of bushy, bumpy ground in Bath Street, up, down, over and round which we used to cycle switchback-style on our daily route from school was a tumbled and overgrown scrap of the town wall and ditch. I did not know that the ridges and furrows on the Bishop's Meadow where we dropped coats while we played football had been dug by the Scots army in its siege of Hereford in 1645. I did not know that The Cut, where I spent much of my earliest playtime, was the cutting of the long- ▷

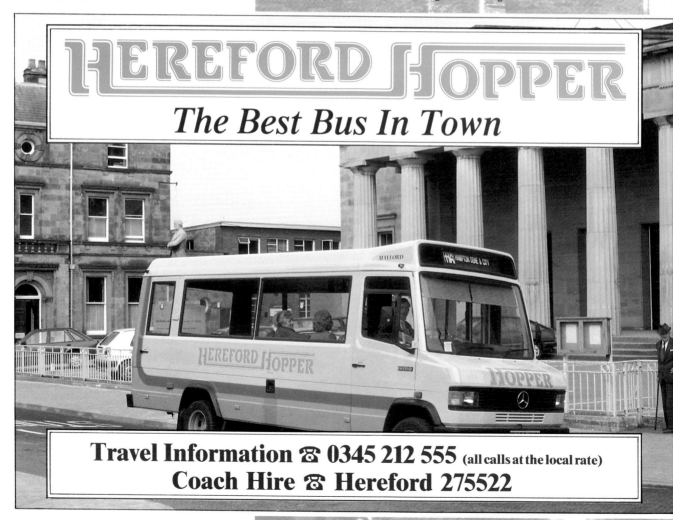

▷ disused Canal Basin or that the timber yard, stacked with huge tree-trunks beneath which my gang made dangerous dens, was the canal wharf itself. The sense of living in a parallel, older Hereford began with an interest in maps, old buildings and sites which grabbed me by the scruff of my neck when I was about ten.

I began to roam the Cathedral and, in particular, the Cloisters at that time, and seem to have been doing so, on and off, ever since. The thrill of contact with the distant past influenced my determination to win a County Scholarship to the dusty old Cathedral School, rather than the brighter, newer High School which many friends preferred - though since I failed the Eleven Plus I didn't have the choice. The Cathedral and the earliest parts of our city fascinated me then and retain a strong hold on my imagination. No surprise to find Hereford and echoes of Hereford appearing frequently in my work: my current commission is for a novel set in the mythical Cathedral city of Archenford in 1916, for instance. (And did you know - the excitement and eagerness - that an Inquisition of Bishops, ordered by the Pope, sat in the North Transept of the Cathedral between August and November of 1307 to examine the miracles claimed at the tomb of Saint Thomas Cantilupe - yes, yes: Cantilupe Street - and authenticated the case of a hanged woman who was returned to life in Saint Martin's Church but commanded the whipping of a dumb boy who had suddenly grown a missing tongue capable of two languages? . . . Sorry . . .)

The Commercial Hotel where I spent my first eighteen years is itself a strange building, surely too high for an inn and originally something completely different - a warehouse, perhaps. Certainly the cavernous cellars were a wonder to me. "Please can I play down the cellar?" must be a comparatively rare request for a small child to make. The position of the pub is interesting, too: opposite the Bus Station which had earlier been the site of the city gaol and, before that, part of Saint Guthlac's Priory. (And did you know that the short, raised section in the centre of the wall dividing the Hospital from the Bus Station is where the gibbet stood, or that it was from the ruins of the medieval Priory that the Parliamentary raiding party raced to hold open Bye Gate at the top of Commercial Street, or Bishop's Street as it was, until a larger force, hidden within two hundred yards of where - eager and excited - I write this now, could reinforce them and take the City in 1645? . . . Sorry . . .)

Accordingly I grew up slowly realising that my roots were deep in a country and city rich with mystery and crowded with ghosts. There is a dark resonance to Hereford that I find both unsettling and reassuring; it's a strange place - good for a writer to live in.

There are a number of things I was never told and wish I had been. I wish I had known, for instance, while reading Marlowe's play, Edward II, for the first time, that the character Despenser, whom the playwright calls 'Spenser', had actually been executed a stone's throw from our classroom, in High Town. I wish I had known - when angrily accused of obstinacy and obstructiveness at my first script conference twenty years ago - that the selfsame complaint about Herefordians in general had been made by Henry VIth in 1438.

And talking about writers, did you know that it was a Hereford Solicitor who penned the popular song of World War One, 'Roses of Picardy' and wrote the words 'Danny Boy' to Percy Grainger's setting of the Londonderry Air and that Percy Grainger's mother kept a shop in Hereford and . . . and . . .

Sorry. □

LEISURE
IN HEREFORD

PROVISION OF PUBLIC SPORTS AND LEISURE FACILITIES

The City Council, in the last 12 years has embarked on an ambitious programme of provision of new sporting and leisure facitlites to meet the needs of the City. The following are the major projects completed in this sphere:-

Hereford Swimming Baths built in 1976 at a cost of £1.5 million and comprising a 25 metre main pool, diving pool, learner pool, squash courts, sauna, solarium, clubroom and cafeteria. The baths has a full programme catering for serious competition, fun swimming, water safety and swimming for exercise and health. Attendances are in excess of 350,000 per annum.

Hereford Municipal Golf course was opened in 1983. Constructed by the Parks labour force at a cost of £87,000 it provides a 9 hole par 4 public Golf course maintained to a very high standard. Rounds played are in excess of 40,000 per annum. Full public tuition facilities are provided by the resident professional.

Hereford Leisure Centre constructed at a cost of £1.3 million officially opened in August 1985. Comprising a large main hall capable of division into 3 separate sections, 4 squash courts, fitness room, changing rooms, meeting room, bar and cafe.

The Leisure Centre offers a full and varied programme of indoor and outdoor sports and entertainments. Attendances are in excess of 250,000 per annum.

The Hereford Athletics Arena adjacent to the Leisure Centre was officially opened in 1988 built at a cost of £400,000 and comprising floodlit 8 lane artificial surfaced track with allied facilities for field events and constructed to International standards, the facility provides high standards for athletics training and competition.

FUTURE SPORTING AND LEISURE PROJECTS

Further sports and leisure schemes are at present either under construction or planned for the near future.

Due for completion by April 1990 are:-

FLOODLIT ARTIFICAL TURF SPORTS PITCH

To be located adjacent to the Leisure Centre at an estimated cost of £300,000 this facility will provide a high standard all weather multi sports surface for competition and training.

SPORTS FIELD AT NEWTON FARM ESTATE

Under construction at an estimated cost of £135,000. This project will provide much needed sports facilities for the South West area of the City.

Due for completion in 1992:-

LEISURE POOL

To be constructed as an addition to the Hereford Swimming Baths at King George VI Playing Fields at an estimated cost of £1 million. The Leisure Pool will be equiped with water slides, fountains and a wave making machine to provide fun for all the family.

MEDIUM TERM PROJECTS

Several medium term projects are being undertaken by the City Council including the development of Dinedor Camp, an ancient hill fort situated 6 miles South of the City, as an area of historic interest and picnic site. Churchill Gardens, surrounding the Museum is gradually being developed as an ornamental garden and arboretum.
The recently produced nature conservation report has been accepted in principle by the City Council. Over the course of the next few years natural areas will be created in the public parks and open spaces in the City, providing havens for wild flowers, insects and small creatures. These areas will help people to understand and respect the natural environment.

W.G. GRACE AND COMPANY PLAYING IN HEREFORD IN 1890.

HEREFORD CRICKET

The Hereford Cricket Club was first established in 1836, with a city and county membership. Tuesdays was practise evening on Widemarsh Common during the Season. The first match was played on Wednesday, 13th July, 1836, between Hereford and Raglan - Hereford was beaten by two wickets. Cricket was popular in the city - £300 was raised by public subscription in 1890, the year Dr. W.G. Grace came to the city with a team of 12 first-rate Gloucestershire cricketers who opposed 18 Herefordshire cricketers captained by Lord Chesterfield, played in atrocious weather: the game ended in a draw.

In 1909, the Cricket Club left the old ground at Widemarsh with its half-timbered pavilion - still there today - and moved to their new ground at the Racecourse, now the Hereford City Sports Club. The City Corporation purchased its Pavilion, and it was a meeting place for local clubs who paid 2 guineas a year for its upkeep. Today, the Herefordshire Cricket Association - the controlling body - promotes interest in the game at all levels within the City and County, and there are now 7 divisions. 46 Clubs take part in the Hereford and District League. Even in winter, cricket interest is maintained in the city through the indoor League - 3 divisions, 24 teams, increasing in popularity every year.

HEREFORD RACECOURSE

There has been a racecourse in Hereford for nearly 400 years. The 1½ mile oval race track was formed in 1774 when the Widemarsh Common was enclosed, however, races had been held on the course for many years before that, but the track was unfenced. As early as 1609, a famous meeting of veteran Morris Dancers took place on the racecourse organised by Sergeant-at-Law John Hoskyns. This was a splendid gathering of twelve ancient cider-drinking Morris Dancers - total ages 1,200 years! ! Many other entertainments were held at the racecourse before racing commenced. In 1819, Tom Spring, later Champion of all England (1823-4) gave an elegant exhibition of boxing.

Advertisements for race meetings can be found in the *Hereford Journal* as early as 1777, although races only took place once a year for three days, usually in August. In 1827, the races had several plates worth £50 each, and special booths were erected for the spectators. Today, fifteen meetings are held each year under National Hunt Rules on the racecourse. Originally, the course crossed Holmer Road, which presumably was closed on race days. The Course attracts good entries and is popular with jockeys, owners and racegoers. All the top riders and horses can be seen, and recently, local jockey, Peter Scudamore, won two races here, and on Easter Monday, 1988, The Princess Royal rode a good third. Grand National Winner, West Tip, had a recent winning outing here at Hereford.

To add to the excellent facilities, plans are under way for a new Grandstand and Members' Enclosure, subject to planning permission.

HEREFORD UNITED

Hereford United is the only Football League club in the county of Herefordshire and Worcestershire and they have enjoyed considerable success since their formation in 1924.

After spells in the Birmingham Combination and the Birmingham League they were elected to the Southern League in 1939 and in the post-war years emerged as one of the country's top non-league clubs.

They beat several league clubs in the F.A. Cup competition and after eliminating First Division Newcastle United in a third round replay, they were elected to the Fourth Division in 1972.

They finished runners-up in the Fourth Division at the first attempt and won the Third Division championship in 1976, attracting gates of over 10,000 for home matches at Edgar Street.

Due to financial problems the club slipped back to the Fourth Division but are looking forward to a brighter future. Hereford United's compact Edgar Street ground is one of the most modern in the lower divisions of the league and the present attendance capacity is 16,119.

RUGBY

Hereford Rugby Club have produced some impressive results in recent seasons after moving from ground to ground during their 120 year history.

The club have now settled at Wyeside, alongside the river, and have merged as one of the most powerful junior clubs in the Midlands.

Following their arrival at Wyeside they won the Central Merit Table three years running and in 1988 they collected the North Midlands Knockout Cup, the West Midlands Floodlight Trophy and the Courage League Midlands Division 2 title.

They also qualified to compete in the Pilkington Cup and after gaining three successive home victories against top junior clubs they were paired with Bath, the most powerful side in the British Isles.

For several weeks they commanded the national headlines and though beaten when they finally went to Bath they gave a gallant display and won many friends.

They draw their players mainly from local schools and run five teams including a successful Colts XV.

HEREFORD ROWING CLUB

Hereford Rowing Club is one of the strongest and wealthiest in the provinces.

Their spacious clubhouse is situated on the north bank of the River Wye which is ideally suited for rowing events. Members travel all over the country to take part in regattas and the haul of trophies they are able to display at the end of each season is the envy of most clubs.

The club hold their own regatta on Whit Monday when oarsmen and oarswomen from all over the country compete in a non-stop 10-hour programme of events. Races are held over 500, 1,000 and 1,500 metres and the regatta is one of the highlights of the city's sporting calendar.

▷

FISHING

> The River Wye is considered to be one of the foremost rivers in the Country for its purity, resulting in it becoming one of the premier salmon rivers in Britain. Trout and coarse fish are also plentiful. The Hereford and District Angling Association controls more than 8 miles of fishing in or near the City, above and below Greyfriars Bridge, as well as extensive water on the River Lugg. Although many of the 'beats' can only be rented on a rod basis for a season, visitor permits are available on a least three good stretches of the water, above and below Hereford and can be obtained from local fishing tackle shops.

A fishing platform for disabled anglers is provided on the bank of the River Wye at the King George V playing field, within easy reach of the City centre.

This beautiful exciting river must have been well used by anglers for sport, and of course food, over the last 800 years. Excavation in the City regularly reveal abundant fishbones, reflecting the excellent diet of Herefordians.! □

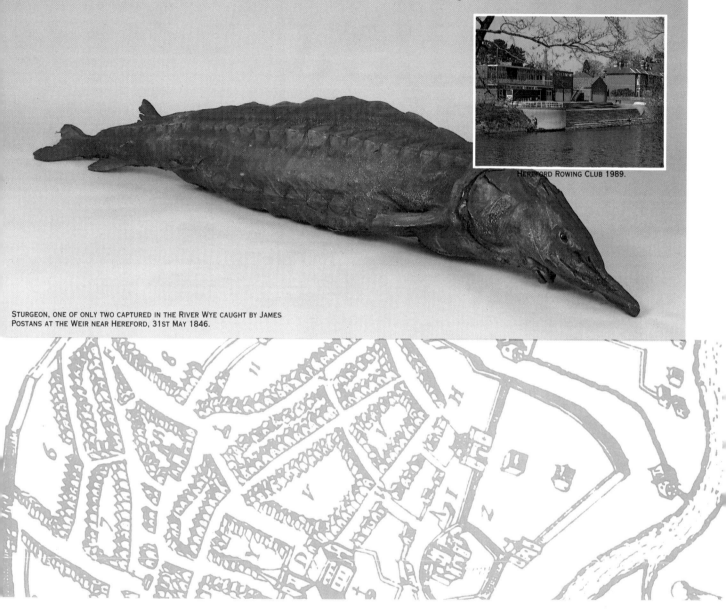

HEREFORD ROWING CLUB 1989.

STURGEON, ONE OF ONLY TWO CAPTURED IN THE RIVER WYE CAUGHT BY JAMES POSTANS AT THE WEIR NEAR HEREFORD, 31ST MAY 1846.

Success, both on and off the field, depends upon teamwork – and that's what we can offer at Sun Valley, being part of a winning team. We are the country's leading producer of fresh and cooked poultry products.

At Sun Valley we give you every opportunity to develop your skills. If you're on the ball you could soon be going for promotion.

To join the team at Sun Valley, just phone Joan Mills on Hereford 59753.

The 10th Anniversary of
The Royal Bank of Scotland in Hereford.
The 800th Anniversary of Hereford.
We are pleased to be associated
with this City.

The Royal Bank of Scotland plc

Paul Roberts, Manager,
21 Broad Street, Hereford HR4 9AP. Tel: 0432 357264.

TOWARDS TOMORROW
FUTURE DEVELOPMENT AND CONSERVATION

During the 800 years since King Richard granted the citizens of Hereford the first opportunities to conduct their own affairs, the fortunes of the city have changed and changed about many times. There was much opulence in the early days of Henry VIII and Hereford in its heyday was called 'the principal city of all the market towns from the sea to the Severn'. When, however, Defoe travelled the County in 1725, he found 'Truly an old, mean built and very dirty city' here. There was no real recovery from this state until the arrival of the railways and the 'Motor Car Age' when expansion got underway for the first time beyond the mediaeval walls. From a population of around 7000 at the start of the 19th Century there was almost a sixfold increase by the middle of the next and the total stood at 40,000 by 1961.

By this time, many parts of the city had again become worn out and bedraggled and in the centre extensive clearance works associated with the major new roadworks of the late 1960's did nothing but good for its appearance.

Fortunately there was no real sacrifice of the stock of heritage buildings or other characteristics leading at that time to Hereford's inclusion in the Council for British Archaeology short list of 51 towns in Britain regarded as 'So splendid and precious that ultimate responsibility for them should be a national concern'.

This was however a time of great vulnerability, for one of the most potent threats to the architectural quality and character of historic towns is from the kind of new shopping and commercial schemes then being devised. Hereford might well have gone the sad way of so many other towns and cities which lost for good such a lot of their intrinsic character in the scramble to substitute generally odious 1960's and 70s 'comprehensive developments'. As it was, major threats did occur but were mostly overcome leaving but a few hideous 'carbuncles' to represent the era. Increasingly since then, conservation policies have developed which, in not seeking to leave everything as it is (often a recipe for neglect), have encouraged design flair and intelligent change for the better - in harmony with the essential nature and 'grain' of the city. 'The Maylord Orchards' shopping and housing scheme, commended regionally, nationally and in Europe 'for the imaginative redevelopment of Hereford's City Centre, providing traditional shopping, parking and residential facilities' is a rewarding recent example of this approach.

The population of the city is now around 49,000, linked with recent annual house completions of up to 400 in local authority, housing association and private sectors (Belmont is outside the city) and by the turn of the century this figure is expected to reach over 51,000. The system for managing such a change has much altered since the days of the small but important 5½ x 4½" document of 1189 and our long series of charters has now been replaced by a bewildering collection of Statutes, Orders and Regulations. Not least are those which enable Herefordians, through an elected District Planning Authority, to work out and then control the ways in which the city is to be shaped and developed. This is through the 'Hereford Local Plan' (price £2.50) which sets out a thorough corporate view of what the City Council is trying to do. Linked to the system under which builders and developers are required to seek planning permission for their schemes, the Plan serves as an authoritative vehicle for future progress. It deals with population and housing, industry and employment, shopping, conservation, building and landscape, transportation, recreation and leisure and social and community facilities. The immediate 10 year period ahead is kept continually under scrutiny and the whole Plan is now under review for extension to 2001.

By then it is thought that some 4,700 new houses will have to be built in and around the city, a majority for local people and the rest for those moving in from other parts of England, notably the South East.

The Local Plan (or District Development Plan as it seems likely to be called in future) will aim to identify suitable land for all these as well as for associated needs such as schools, further industry, shopping, recreational space and so on.

It will provide an essential thorough corporate view of everything the community wishes to do, and see done, during the approach to 2001 so that the City of Hereford will be well placed to meet the challenges and opportunities of the new century and a further millenium of dynamic history.

□

THE FUTURE OF LEISURE AND TOURISM IN HEREFORD

The current policy of Hereford City Council is to offer every member of the local population the opportunity to enjoy art and sporting facilities at whatever level they choose. People generally have more free time, and are more affluent, than at any period in our history. There is also an increasing awareness of the importance of physical fitness. Initiatives by the Sports Council, locally, regionally and nationally are developing the concept of *"Sport for All"* - especially targeting young people and women. The patriotic would like to see more British sporting success; there is a demand for a more aggressive pursuit of excellence. Improving medical care, and a reduction in the birth rate is resulting in an increasingly older population. With these considerations in mind, the City Council is currently involved in promoting the "XL Initiative" offering the very best of available coaching instruction to promising youngsters and leading a "Community Sports 50 Plus Leader Course", to develop skills for those involved in encouraging the 50 plus age group to participate in sporting activity. Possible similar courses to cater for the 70 plus age group will be the next step.

Facilities for organised sport in Hereford are now excellent. The River Wye and surrounding countryside offer ample opportunities for those who prefer less formal rural activity. Those who are responsible for the development of such facilities will in the future have to satisfy the growing demands of the differing sports, from the very popular and profitable, to the minority and unprofitable, and balance the demand for excellence against the desire for mass participation. Hereford is fortunate in enjoying an   ▷

CHURCH STREET

active arts environment encompassing music, theatre, film, visual arts, craft and community arts. The New Hereford Theatre, Cathedral and Leisure Centre together with smaller facilities available throughout the City offer venues suitable for the presentation of a wide variety of amateur and professional productions. In recognising the aspirations of local residents the Council recently adopted an *"Arts for All"* policy, increased funding for the arts, and appointed an Arts Development Officer to develop the policy. Improved facilities, better co-ordination, promotion and marketing of arts events will result in a greater awareness by the local population of the opportunities currently available. This should be translated into greater public involvement, both in active participation and as spectators, which in turn will hopefully provide the impetus to generate even more interest. Given the present enthusiasm and commitment properly harnessed, the City can look forward to a stimulating, exciting and vibrant arts future.

Hereford, an ancient city on the banks of the Wye, set amid beautiful countryside is ideally situated to take full advantage of the economic benefits to be derived from tourism. The continually increasing number of enquiries received by the Tourist Information Centre provides evidence that the current policy of promoting Hereford as an attractive location for a short break or day out is proving very successful.

The Marches area, where England and Wales meet, should be given a higher profile and promoted to encourage longer holidays, activity or special interest breaks, conferences and could successfully compete for a greater share of the overseas market. The challenge for the future will be to promote Hereford as a major tourist centre of the Marches while ensuring the City retains its own unique identity and quality of life long enjoyed by its residents.

HEREFORD A CENTRE FOR TOURISM

Hereford is ideally located for the visitor to make it a touring base to see the rest of the Shire.

Near the city, amongst the orchards, hop fields and meadows of low land Herefordshire are some of England's prettiest black and white villages - places like Eardisland, Pembridge and Weobley, world famous examples of traditional English villages with a wealth of timber framed buildings. There is a vast selection of places to see within an hour's drive. To the West lies Offa's Dyke and the "Kilvert Country" around the Welsh border town of Hay on Wye, home of the world's largest second hand bookshop. Nearby are the Black Mountains and the Golden Valley.

South of the City is the marvellous Norman church of Kilpeck, Ross on Wye, and the Forest of Dean, with its silent woodland trails, while to the East lies Elgar country, the bare Malverns and the hills around the Teme Valley with their quiet lanes and hamlets. To the North are Leominster and Ludlow, two charming market towns, and the Shropshire hills which lead Westward into Wales, towards the source of the Wye and Severn rivers. The proximity of the Welsh border, and the constant fear of attack, led to the building of a tremendous number of castles in the County. Over ninety have been identified, ranging from powerful fortresses like Goodrich and great baronial strongholds such as Wigmore, to the humble mounds which originally had wooden towers and defences. Many of these saw their last action during the Civil War and they repay a visit. Throughout history, Hereford has been a key visitor centre for the Wye Tour, particularly in the 18th century, and during the 19th century, much beloved by the Victorians who toured the delights of the area by rail. Today visitors still come by rail, but mainly by car and coach to enjoy the Capital of the Marches.

THE GARDENS NEAR THE VICTORIA BRIDGE.

Her Majesty the Queen leaving the Old House on her visit to the city on 15th April, 1976 to distribute the Royal Maundy.

ACKNOWLEDGEMENTS

The Editor gratefully thanks all the contributors to this commemorative book:-

Sue Hubbard, Ron Shoesmith, Richard Morriss, Graham J. Roberts, Stuart P. Gent, Ray Boddington, Jacob O'Callaghan, Jean O'Donnell, G. E. Forrest, Tony Carr, Richard Shields, F. H. H. Pilkington, Terry Court, Richard J. Grainger, John Harnden, B. J. Whitehouse, Col. T. J. B. Hill, Basil Butcher, Alick Rowe, Jim Fisk, J. D. Simmons, Geoff Cole, John Oldman, Ted Woodriffe.

Very many thanks for photography are especially due to *Ken Hovard and Jenny Houston*, and also *Richard Hammonds.*

Similarly, I am grateful for loan of photographic material and permission to obtain photographs; Hereford City Library (Mr. B. J. Whitehouse and his staff), Miss S. Hubbard (County Record Office), Mr. E. Hatton, Mr. R. Shoesmith and Col. T. J. B. Hill, the Right Reverend the Lord Bishop of Hereford, John Eastaugh.

Many of the photographs are taken from the City Museum's collection, whilst others have been specially commissioned for this book. Every effort has been made to ascertain photographic copyright where appropriate.

Finally, very special thanks are due to Jean Goode and Eve Finney and to Althea Brown and Keith Martin of Revelstone Publishing.